FROM
SOURCE
TO SOLD

Published by Grammar Factory Publishing, an imprint of MacMillan Company Limited.

Grammar Factory Publishing
MacMillan Company Limited
25 Telegram Mews, 39th Floor, Suite 3906
Toronto, Ontario, Canada
M5V 3Z1

www.grammarfactory.com

Palamariu, Radu, 1984–
Alicke, Knut, 1968–
    From Source to Sold: Stories of Leadership in Supply Chain / Radu Palamariu and Knut Alicke.

Paperback ISBN 978-1-98973-789-7
Hardcover ISBN 978-1-98973-791-0
eBook ISBN 978-1-98973-790-3

    1. BUS116000 BUSINESS & ECONOMICS / Logistics & Supply Chain. 2. BUS071000 BUSINESS & ECONOMICS / Leadership. 3. BUS012000 BUSINESS & ECONOMICS / Careers / General.

Production Credits
Cover design by Designerbility
Interior layout design by Dania Zafar
Book production and editorial services by Grammar Factory Publishing

Grammar Factory's Carbon Neutral Publishing Commitment
Grammar Factory Publishing is proud to be neutralizing the carbon footprint of all printed copies of its authors' books printed by or ordered directly through Grammar Factory or its affiliated companies through the purchase of Gold Standard-Certified International Offsets.

Disclaimer

FROM
SOURCE
TO SOLD

STORIES OF LEADERSHIP IN SUPPLY CHAIN

RADU PALAMARIU AND
KNUT ALICKE

CONTENTS

INTRODUCTION

"Why don't we see more supply chain leaders becoming CEOs?"

This was the question that, twelve months ago, put us on the road to this book.

Usually, the only kind of attention supply chain gets is negative. If an order isn't manufactured, shipped, and/or delivered on time, supply chain is where the fingers start pointing. But in 2020, as COVID-19 took hold around the world, the often-invisible work of supply chain became a matter of both intense public interest and boardroom gratitude.

When resource scarcity, workforce shortages and transportation bottlenecks hit hard, it was supply chain experts who kept supermarket shelves stocked with food and stopped businesses' bottom lines from plummeting. And as more and more disruptions followed on the heels of the pandemic — the semiconductor shortage, the reduction in rubber and lumber production, the Russian invasion of Ukraine — it became apparent that it was supply chain that kept the world moving in times of chaos.

So, if supply chain leaders have proven time and again that they can successfully steer the ship through a crisis, why aren't more of them captaining the ship permanently — from the CEO's desk?

If you're in supply chain, you probably think you know the answer. We supply chain people tend to be pragmatic, can-do types. We love our data and number-crunching. We prefer to get the job done properly rather than rushing to look good at the end of a quarter. CEOs and top-executive types are "visionaries"; supply chain professionals prefer the view from the ground.

But what if we told you that your view from the ground gives you the clearest and furthest-reaching vision of all? That the processes you work every day to perfect are the key to your organization's stability and sustainability? And that the resilience you look to build into the system is the biggest kind of thinking there is, because it will safeguard your business against an ever more disruptive future?

This is the reason we created this book. In our respective and varied experiences within the industry — whether as consultant, connector, recruiter, professor, educator, and even podcast host — we've encountered so many supply chain leaders who have the creativity, competency, and vision that are crucial for chief or senior executive positions, but who haven't (yet) reached those peaks simply because the possibility never occurred to them.

So, we thought: what better way to awaken all of these people to their untapped potential than to speak with some of the most successful and accomplished top-level supply chain leaders in the world — to have those leaders tell the stories of their career journeys and describe their leadership styles in their own words.

In *From Source to Sold*, you'll hear from more than two dozen top supply chain leaders, working across eleven countries and in industries that range from massive multinationals to innovative start-ups. You'll learn about the experiences that allowed them to develop their skills. You'll observe the qualities that helped single them out as leadership material. And, perhaps most importantly, you'll discover their tips and techniques for clearly and powerfully *communicating* both the vision of their organization, and supply chain's role within that vision, up and down the company ladder.

At a time when supply chain is growing as never before — with more MBAs being taken in supply chain than in finance, and with more and more young people entering the industry with the digital skills that can equip supply chain for the challenges of a uniquely disruptive century — this book spotlights a variety of role models who can provide inspiration and guidance for your career journey through this challenging, dynamic, and incredibly rewarding field. Whether you are just starting out in supply chain, or are an established supply chain leader looking to make the leap to the C-suite, these lessons in leadership will give you a clearer and brighter view of the road ahead.

—RADU PALAMARIU & KNUT ALICKE

PRELUDE:
RADU PALAMARIU & KNUT ALICKE

"You've got to ask yourself in every role: 'How can I add more value, and what's the most value that I can add?'"

One of the reasons we wanted to collaborate on this book is that we have each had very different experiences within and approaches to supply chain — which, we believe, helps give extra strength to the many views we share on it, the conclusions we've drawn, and the hopes we have for the field as a whole.

So before we launch into the conversations we had with some of the top names in supply chain, we sat down for this two-headed "self-interview" to talk a little about our own journeys in the industry, where we think it is today, and why we believe that supply chain is uniquely equipped to breed the organizational leaders of the future.

What were your respective entries into the supply chain field, and how did your journeys influence the way you view the industry?

Radu Palamariu: Randomness, really! I graduated with a degree in psychology, and for about ten years had several roles in management consulting, training and development. Then I became part of an executive search firm that had just opened up its office in Singapore, and I ended up being focused on supply chain because one of the firm's first big clients was in supply chain. So you can rightfully say that I "fell into it."

And in all honesty, at the beginning, I had no clue what "supply chain" meant — I hadn't even heard the term. And because I felt like I could not add value as a headhunter if I didn't know the sector, I tried to read as much on it as I could. The first supply chain books — written by two of the best minds in the industry, Yossi Sheffi (one of the contributors to this book) and John Gattorna — were a revelation for me. They showed me that the whole world is a supply chain — everything ever produced is part of the supply chain.

They also showed me that, when you remove the technical jargon, supply chain is about people. As the years went by, I got more and more fascinated by the people who work in supply chain. From aviation and shipping professionals, to couriers and postal workers, from production experts to manufacturing engineers, from buyers and planners to procurement and logistics, all of these are truly the people that keep the world moving. They get our food to us; they make sure every parcel we order online finds its way to our door; they create and deliver the vital medical supplies we need.

And, by and large, they all share certain key characteristics: they're down to earth, pragmatic, and really about getting shit done. But one thing they're generally *not* about is talking to others loudly and clearly about what they do — sharing supply chain values with the rest of the organization and educating people about why supply chain is so key. And that, of course, was one of the driving purposes behind this book.

Knut Alicke: In my case, I first got involved with supply chain management when I was doing my PhD in mechanical engineering. This was after I'd given up on my first ambition, which was to be a musician — I actually studied to be a jazz saxophonist, but after I realized what it takes to be a genius in music, I decided that I should go back to my dry old mechanical engineering roots!

When I was doing my PhD, what really excited me was complex systems, and supply chain was the perfect playing field for exploring those — particularly because it allowed me to put what I was studying into practice. What often happens in university is that you spend your time devising theoretical models that are nice to publish, but have no practical application at all. Supply chain allowed me to solve real problems within real complex systems, which I found super-exciting — and I still do, both when I'm working with clients at McKinsey, or teaching students about supply chain management in a classroom setting.

Shuttling back and forth between the industry and academia has really made it clear that there's a big gap between what academia *thinks* is done in practice and what is really done in practice. And, on the other side, a lot of the industry doesn't use the kind of theoretical models that would allow them to function more efficiently. Many times, when talking with clients about how they calculate optimal inventory levels, I'll start writing down formulas on a flip chart, and they find this just amazing.

So to me, it's really about bridging that gap: of bringing the practical stuff into the lecture hall and incorporating it with the theory, and bringing theoretical *tools* — not "theory" as an insular, self-contained system — into the practical stuff. This is the missing link.

Why do you think that supply chain hasn't yet become the "breeding ground" for future top leaders the way that some other fields have?

Knut Alicke: I think some of it comes from the fact that, when you come right down to it, the field itself is relatively new. In something like accounting, which has been around for hundreds of years, you have international standards. Manufacturing, as well, is much older than supply chain, and has production models that are similar all over the world, given that Toyota's production system has become the quasi-standard.

Now, you could argue that supply chain is comparable to those fields because it had its base in logistics, and logistics came out of the military — ensuring soldiers are supplied with everything they need for the battlefield and all that. So if you take that view, supply chain is hundreds of years old at this point.

But in reality, the whole *planning* aspect of supply chain is still relatively new, because it came from two developments that only emerged about thirty years ago. First, there was the wider availability of computers, which meant that you could quickly and accurately perform calculations that were previously done manually. Second, the rise of globalization and outsourcing meant that supply chain now had to manage a whole *network* to get the product from customer to supplier, not just maintain a physical flow as in the logistics days.

So in my opinion, if you're talking about supply chain in the truly *contemporary* meaning of the term, I'd say that it's *progressing*, but it's not yet mature. And the fact that it doesn't yet have the same kind of well-established and clearly understood function as accounting, or manufacturing, or sales, means that the board is less likely to look to it when asking who the leaders of the next generation are going to be.

Radu Palamariu: And that leads right into the definitional aspect — by which I mean, depending on who you ask, "supply chain" can mean all manner of different things.

For me, the simplest and clearest definition of supply chain is the Supply Chain Operations Reference (SCOR) model: Plan, Source, Make, Deliver, and Return. These are the five pillars of any company that makes products, and supply chain is what connects them. But when you look at a range of companies, you'll see that they have all kinds of different structures.

For example, sometimes procurement is under supply chain, or sometimes it's completely separate, depending on whether it's a service company or a manufacturing company. In the last year, I was recruiting a regional chief supply chain officer (CSCO) for a large FMCG company, and they don't even *call* the role a CSCO – they call it VP of operations. So across industries, there's not even a common, agreed-upon definition of what supply chain is and does.

Do you think, then, that it's possible to have a unified system of supply chain that can be applied across all manner of different industries, similar to the way it has been for areas like manufacturing, sales, etc.?

Knut Alicke: This is something we wanted to understand in a survey we did at McKinsey[1]: is there a best-practice organizational structure for supply chain? How much do you integrate into supply chain? Is procurement in? Is manufacturing? Is it only planning and logistics? Is it everything? And then, if you're considering companies that operate globally, how much should be centralized and how much should be delegated regionally?

And what was interesting in our results was, after correlating organizational structures with performance (for which we used EBITDA as a very simple proxy), there are super-successful companies that are completely integrated, and other super-successful companies that are non-integrated; some of them are completely centralized, some are completely decentralized. So what we concluded is that, really, there is no one best practice — what you need to do is optimally apply your resources for your specific purpose.

Radu Palamariu: To make a probably way too simple analogy out of Knut's answer, you could say that supply chain is like a Lego kit — not one of the kits where you're supposed to follow the instruction book to build one specific thing, but a standard kit, with a whole array of different blocks, figures, wheels, etc.

---

1 https://www.mckinsey.com/business-functions/operations/our-insights/how-great-supply-chain-organizations-work

What a kit like that allows you to do is build whatever you want to build with the Lego that you have. So if you're into building trucks, you can build trucks; if you want to build a house, you can make a house; if you're into army vehicles, you build a tank. It all starts with the same pool of materials, but you need to design it to fit your own purposes.

Given all this, then, do you still think that supply chain is a field that can equip people with the knowledge and experience they need to take on higher, executive-level roles?

Radu Palamariu: Of course! If we say that supply chain is the nervous system of a company, then it only makes sense that successful supply chain leaders have the ability to direct that company. When you're in supply chain, you're moving three things: you're moving goods, you're moving information, and you're moving money. These are, more or less, the crucial elements of any company. So if you're the one orchestrating all that movement, it only makes sense that you've got C-suite potential, because you're seeing everything, every day.

And I think that why we haven't yet seen quite so many supply chain leaders make that leap is because of what I said about them before: they tend to be more pragmatic, get-it-done types who don't know how to "sell themselves" and communicate that big, overarching vision they have in a way that goes beyond the nuts and bolts.

Knut Alicke: Not to pick on sales types, but a comparison I like to make is that a sales person will crow that "I made this one order," and not mention the nine other orders that they missed; a supply chain person will confess, "I missed this one order," and not tell you about the nine they delivered on time.

That's obviously painting the situation with way too broad a brush, but I do think it speaks to the kind of culture and mindset that many supply chain people ingrained in themselves. And I think that, to a certain extent, that self-perception bled over into the outlook of the wider company as well.

Many years ago I did a workshop with the supply chain leadership team at a large company, where we talked about career progression. It turned out that this company had their model and program for developing future leaders, and supply chain was simply not included. The attitude from the top seemed to be, "if you have a manufacturing background, or an R&D background, or a sales or marketing background, you qualify for a board position, but not if you have a supply chain background."

However, while I think that we're still somewhat living in the "hangover" of that period, things are changing. In the past, we would often have people who were demand planners who were happy to just be demand planners for the next thirty years, because the culture around them didn't really enable the kind of entrepreneurial spirit you need to grow yourself and your career. But in the last few years, everyone is talking about supply chain — CEOs are saying "Wow, supply chain just saved us!" And I think that people in supply chain are starting to realize that they can not only change something for the better within their own field, but also on a broader scope for their company as a whole.

So do you think, then, that it's just a question of supply chain leaders "waking up" to their exec-level potential?

Radu Palamariu: Obviously, there are some "soft" skills that supply chain leaders — or leaders in any field — need to hone: they need to get better at presentation skills, at influencing skills, etc. But I do think that the first and most important thing is that they *believe* they have this potential. And as we are now seeing more supply chain people climbing higher than they have before, that's going to set off a domino effect.

Let me give you an example of what I mean. For a long time, everyone thought that no human could ever run a four-minute mile. They even had scientific studies showing that this was physically impossible. And then, in the 1950s, this guy Roger Bannister did it — he ran a mile in under four minutes. And not two months later, another guy broke *that* record. And today, you have like 1,500 people who have done it, all because this one original guy went and showed that it was possible.

I think that the same principle can apply in supply chain. Once people know that something has been done, that it's possible to do, you're going to see more and more people doing it. It's the basic law of attraction.

But of course, just like not every person can now run a four-minute-mile, probably not every supply chain leader is going to have real senior-executive potential. What would you say are some of the intrinsic qualities or principles of supply chain leaders who have made it to that level?

Knut Alicke: As you'll see from the conversations with the people in this book, what they all have is a certain level of humility: if we had asked any of them, "Did you plan your career to become a CEO?" they would all say no. But what eventually gave them that opportunity is that, even though most of them are very analytic, "numbers people," they also have an innate sense of how to lead *humans*, not just resources. They listen, they're open to feedback, and most importantly they have a... *vision* always sounds a little pretentious, in my opinion, but they have *something* that they want their companies to achieve. And that fundamental humility opens the door for them to better relate to people, and motivate them to strive for that goal together.

Radu Palamariu: Just as we were saying earlier that there is no one best practice in terms of supply chain operations, I think that if there's one thing everyone should take away from this book, it's that there's no one way to make that career leap — if not all, then there are at least many roads that lead to Rome. So to build on what Knut just said, I think it's key to be flexible in your view of your career progress. It's not necessarily about thinking that you must always be taking steps up...that your career needs to be linear — because especially in today's world, it won't be. Instead, you've got to be open to taking side steps, and not regarding them as a "waiting room" — you've got to ask yourself in every role, "How can I add more value, and what's the most value that I can add?"

But of course there is a second level to that, because even if you're adding value that doesn't mean you're going to get noticed for it. So that's where you do need to learn about the communication aspect — the storytelling, the influencing, *showing* people how what you're doing is adding value. And this is something that, by and large, supply chain folks are not really doing.

Knut Alicke: But the people we spoke to for this book are all excellent at that. Some were maybe born with it, others learned it, but they can all *do* it, and that – combined, of course, with being excellent at their jobs – is what has allowed them to make that leap.

Radu Palamariu: When you get down to it, life is simple – we just overcomplicate things by thinking that there's some sort of secret sauce. There isn't! There are just principles, qualities, experiences, like Knut said. And it's what you draw from these, and how you apply them, that will help determine the path you take.

EDITOR'S NOTE

The idea behind this book was clear from the onset: to amplify the voices of the leaders running supply chains of businesses that touch millions of lives every day. My task was to help draw out the fascinating and insightful stories of their experiences in the supply chain field without straying too far into technical jargon or academic theory.

Structuring the interviews took some effort. Although we distributed a standardized questionnaire to our contributors, the responses that we gleaned from these were always intended to simply set the guidelines for later, more in-depth conversations. For these, Radu and Knut wanted to create a genuinely interactive, conversational atmosphere, as we all believed that this approach would unearth more vibrant stories from our contributors — particularly as all the interviews would have to be conducted remotely.

This theory proved to be true as we set about conducting our twenty-six interviews throughout the latter half of 2021 and early 2022. We would initiate conversations on a lighter note, discussing current developments at the contributor's work; mentioning the pandemic would often elicit particularly animated responses from our interviewees, and help set the tone for what followed. By letting the discussions go where they would, we found that our interviewees would often surprise us by leading the dialogue down intriguing paths we never could have expected. Even contributors who have been interviewed many times before for many other outlets remarked that some of the things they told us here, they had never spoken about publicly before!

These conversations are now collected in the book you hold, each one filled with invaluable insights and incredible anecdotes about the tightrope-walking these leaders have had to do to keep their supply chains up and running 24/7. Happy reading!

—VISHNU RAJAMANICKAM

CHAPTER 1:

VIKRAM AGARWAL

"In the end, success in the supply chain boils down to just two aspects: value creation and authentic leadership."

Vikram Agarwal is the COO of Danone, spearheading end-to-end supply chain operations from the company's head office in Paris. He has more than thirty years of experience in the global supply chain, working across Asia, Europe and Africa in various leadership capacities for several highly reputed FMCG companies, including Unilever (where he spent a total of thirty years), Avon, and Dole.

Vikram Agarwal's first significant exposure to supply chain leadership came in 1997, when he was appointed to lead a multifunctional team and a few hundred employees, as a factory manager. "Heading a factory comes with responsibility," Agarwal attests. "On one hand, you've got to maintain productivity to deliver business goals. At the same time, it is necessary to invest in good employee relations, keep up the motivational levels, and ensure care for all employees." Considering that a factory is ground zero of the extended supply chain, and its health impacts that of the rest of the business either positively or adversely, the assignment proved to be a trial by fire, and Agarwal contends that this early test helped him build the leadership acumen he possesses now.

"The next inflection point in my career came when I took up the role of the vice president of procurement for Asia-Africa at Unilever,"

Agarwal continues. "While I was used to dealing with people when handling operations at the ground level as a factory manager, that was in a controlled and structured environment. My position in procurement brought home the understanding of the external world.

"[Procurement] is about dealing with suppliers whose business interests, at least in theory, are in conflict with ours," Agarwal says. "One has to constantly find the win–win spot which allows for strategic growth on both sides, fosters a long-term relationship, and at the same time keeps us cost-competitive. Walking this ledge successfully is a necessary skill that every supply chain leader needs to pick up."

When Agarwal moved from Unilever to Avon as chief supply chain officer on the company executive committee, the biggest change he had to become accustomed to was the substantially scaled-down operations and, consequently, the need to manage financial metrics differently in a company that was one-tenth the size of his former employer. "At Unilever cash was not something we worried about, as we had a cash surplus managed effectively by a corporate treasury function," relates Agarwal. "At Avon, cash needed to be managed by every leader in the supply chain through major operational drivers such as working capital and Capex, which needed constant attention on an ongoing basis.

"It was an entirely different paradigm operating in a small company versus a larger, more secure one, which introduced a new realization around the value of cash management and return on invested capital."

KEEPING IT SIMPLE TO SOLVE COMPLICATED SUPPLY CHAIN PROBLEMS

After decades of experience at the helm of the supply chain, Agarwal has distilled the nitty-gritty of doing business down to three simple things: "revenue growth, profitability, and cash. Any business across the world largely revolves around these three parameters. In the supply chain, we need to constantly connect our actions with these business imperatives," he declares.

"Not making this connection results in the disorientation of teams. For instance, when we fill trucks more, make them run longer or faster, or do multi-drops, we should be able to link these actions with business values. It is about reducing costs to improve profitability, lowering inventory to increase cash, or bettering customer service to grow revenue. The drive and motivational levels of operating managers shift completely when the positive impact of their actions is seen in the business results."

As a negative example of this dynamic, Agarwal points out how improving a factory's overall equipment effectiveness (OEE) would not directly translate into business values unless the higher productivity is leveraged to either trim down factory fixed operating costs, or avoid the need for more Capex to create additional capacity. In Agarwal's analogy, this would be like creating a supercar that cannot serve the purpose of taking us from point A to B.

Explaining the supply chain in business terms to peers in the organization and on the board is critical, Agarwal stresses. And further, translating supply chain issues into a language that businesspeople from outside the industry can also fathom is an essential part of being a leader. "In the supply chain we often talk supply chain jargon and set KPIs without translating them into what they mean for the business around three basic dimensions: growth, profitability, and cash," Agarwal states. "It is important to not let supply chains work for supply chains.

"I break operations down to the primary components of plan, make, source, and deliver. Start with delivery to the consumer or customer, plan the way back to 'make,' and then source the materials flow. Each leg needs to contribute to one or more of the three business dimensions. It just keeps everything simple."

From his days as a factory manager right up to today, Agarwal continues to believe that factories speak to the overall health of the extended supply chain. "For instance, I often start a factory tour from the raw and pack materials warehouse. Some find this quite unconventional, but looking closely at the material packaging in the racks gives a fair idea of the proximity of the suppliers and the import components — especially in developing markets — and the degree of over-specification of the materials. Similarly, the weekly truck placements are indicative of the customer demand and distribution trend. Asking the drivers the distance to their last station before they came to pick up this load gives a fair idea of the truck availability situation.

"I put factories in two categories," Agarwal continues. "A factory can either be a 'thinking factory' or a 'walking factory.' In a thinking factory, one can spot creative solutions — they are physical and visible, and don't need hand-holding via PowerPoint. A walking factory is just manning, perhaps over-manning, the machines. The difference is morale and effective leadership."

MAKING A CASE FOR SUPPLY CHAIN RESILIENCE IN A CHAOTIC WORLD

When Agarwal joined Danone in early 2022, the company was already in the midst of fighting the pandemic's aftereffects on its supply chains from the frequent industrial stoppages up the chain. When Russia invaded Ukraine shortly thereafter, Agarwal realized that this was a crucial time for the business. With a large supply base in Europe, the war created a whiplash effect that caused disruption and high inflation not seen for a very long time.

"My team has needed to push constantly for more resilience in the supply base, across our operations, upstream suppliers, and downstream transporters," Agarwal says. "Risk forecasting and resilience planning in the supply chain have become vital in the post-COVID era. The pandemic only triggered it, though — the black swan events that have followed since have forced us to operate in a completely new business environment."

While supply chains have become progressively more efficient at managing huge throughputs, a small disruption has the capability of throwing this large-scale machinery out of gear. Now, the time-tested practice of just-in-time procurement is transitioning to just-in-case models that offer more stability to operations. This brings with it the need for a deeper and broader vendor base. "A highly concentrated vendor base relying on single-supplier, single-factory scale to create cost efficiencies is showing up as a high-risk area," Agarwal says. "Material specifications that allow supplier homologation around different parts of the world are one means of mitigating this risk, as industrial disruptions usually have a regional footprint.

"Building resilience by going deeper and broader into the supply chain base has become key to sustaining operations in the post-pandemic era," he continues. "For instance, to overcome the container sea freight crisis, a few companies are going the extra mile by chartering break-bulk vessels. They would rather take a vessel and run it empty one way across the ocean than struggle to secure containers on that elusive vessel at a high cost and still risk long delays at congested terminals and increased journey times."

Agarwal asserts that companies should stop looking at supply chain operations as stand-alone entities and see them as a piece in the overall business puzzle. "Supply chain professionals should work for the business, and not the supply chain itself. I always ask people to avoid doing things that are not business-relevant. For instance, don't over-specify infrastructure while building a new factory when the product doesn't require it. It will only make it more unwieldy to change course when change comes."

RESPONDING TO CRISES WITH OUT-OF-THE-BOX SOLUTIONS

Even though disruptions are becoming more commonplace in the industry, firefighting operational issues has always been part of the job description of a supply chain leader. But for his part, Agarwal prefers to focus on out-of-the-box thinking during a crisis situation, as this leads to the creation of more business value.

By way of example, Agarwal cites an anecdote from his time at Unilever. "When I was leading procurement for Asia and Africa, there was a movement by some NGOs against FMCG companies using palm oil in their products, which gained momentum with consumers in Europe on the grounds that the palm oil industry was causing mass-scale deforestation and social exploitation. This started affecting revenues. We decided to investigate, and found there was some circumstantial evidence of such instances with one of our major suppliers in Southeast Asia."

This led the company to discontinue sourcing from that supplier, creating a cascade effect that saw other FMCG companies delisting liable suppliers. As the delisting snowballed, the supply chain of one of the largest commodities in the world — palm oil — became unstable.

"We went out of stock. We had to patiently work through palm oil producer industry bodies, individual producers, NGOs, governments, media, new legislation, and our FMCG counterparts to resolve the situation, without compromising our position on sustainability, since it was a principled stand we had taken publicly," Agarwal relates. "It took one year of intensive work to restore supply stability."

However, this effort had a positive consequence. "Managing this crisis enabled me to have a closer look at the upstream and down-stream economics of the palm oil oleochemical industry. I realized that, as a buyer, we would soon be squeezed by producers' and refiners' rising margins. On the other hand, the pricing power for palm oil-based products in our major markets was limited due to the anti-palm oil movement. We were headed for a margin squeeze."

After much thought, Agarwal decided that it was time for Unilever to set up its own facility for a substantial part of its volume requirements to create a credible hedge against this oncoming squeeze, and go upstream right to the farm to ensure traceability of certified sustainable palm oil. It was a difficult proposal to obtain agreement upon internally, since the company had veered away from investments in non-core products.

"We did receive permission, but it came with stiff conditions on achieving sustainable sourcing and receiving incentives from the Indonesian government. It took us three years to negotiate these incentives, set up the inbound supplies, and build a large oleochemicals complex," Agarwal says. "During this period, we fought internal doubts about this being a feasible venture, while facing a hardening stance from current oleochemical suppliers where we weren't welcome any longer. Finally, we got there. And over the last five years, this facility has created huge value for the company."

Another incident at Unilever where Agarwal's forward-thinking decisions made a significant difference was when he found himself in the middle of a tea plantation sale in East Africa. "I was briefed on the decision to dispose of the plantation — a decision that had already been made due to financial unviability and intense pressure from some European NGOs on the socio-environmental impact of the operations," he remembers.

But when Agarwal visited the site, he realized it was actually a well-established operation spread over thousands of hectares where close to 10,000 people worked. "The reasons for poor financial performance lay in inefficiencies that could be corrected. I figured the environmental impact could actually be turned positive with a few interventions. The alternative of course was to close operations, which would see people lose their livelihoods."

Furthermore, the plant contained an ancient forest reserve with a very delicate ecosystem. "We were not only caring for it, but also protecting it from illegal poachers and loggers. If we were to exit the scene, it was only a matter of time before this would be completely destroyed by a hapless community deprived of their livelihood. In short, us leaving would have turned the entire area into a wasteland.

"It was a long story thereafter: first about internal persuasion against selling, then developing a recovery plan, getting some of the world's best experts into the middle of nowhere, and finally an economic turnaround. These plantations are today a valuable asset, not just for the owners but also for the countries involved."

THE NO-NONSENSE APPROACH TO
SUPPLY CHAIN LEADERSHIP

When it comes to recruitment, Agarwal declares that he would always pick a person with the hunger to "fill the glass" rather than someone who would happily accept a glass half full. "I look for people who have a can-do attitude without being reckless, because it's easy to say no when working in the supply chain. 'Can the factory increase its production in the next month?' 'Can you reduce people in distribution by 30 percent this year?' 'Can you launch this new product in six months' time?' 'Can you supply this unplanned customer order in two days?' The usual answer to all these questions is no, so I often flip the question and ask them what it would take for them to say yes.

"For me, it's important that the person I'm working with is capable of going from 'it can't be done' to 'what does it take to get it done?' There is always a solution, a workaround, especially in the supply chain, to reach an acceptable outcome."

Leadership potential is the next attribute on the list of what Agarwal looks for when hiring. In the FMCG industry, typically 25 percent to 30 percent of the workforce would be in the supply chain, which makes it crucial to have leaders who can communicate clearly to their people and lead large teams with a common strategy. "Authentic leadership is crucial, even more so when dealing with people in the warehouse or factory shop floor. People seek for you to be inspirational and caring, not just in speech but in all your actions. A supply chain leader is as visible as a goldfish in a bowl — more so than other functions, due to [the fact that they have] more encounters with people on the ground. Great PowerPoint presentations are not assets for these people — they need to sense your personal direction and authenticity."

> "It's important that the person I'm working with is capable of going from 'it can't be done' to 'what does it take to get it done?' There is always a solution, a workaround, especially in the supply chain, to reach an acceptable outcome."

Agarwal also advises that "a role in the supply chain requires you to participate in almost every business discussion, so you need to develop the business acumen to engage in these constructively. Although some may seem removed from operations, like a discussion on future market share trends, it actually would have a bearing on your capacity planning."

The trick to being a good supply chain professional is to connect both ends of the spectrum — the business aspect and the physical product flow aspect. "Nobody will instruct you to establish a new factory or distribution center or enhance supplier capacity. You will have to develop the capability to understand short- and long-term demand sensing," Agarwal says. "And it is a decision with consequences — if you get it right, it creates value for the business. If not, it leads to impairments. In the end, success in the supply chain boils down to just two aspects: value creation and authentic leadership."

Scan the QR code below or visit www.sourcetosold.com to access exclusive bonus content you can use with your teams to further explore the concepts and insights covered in this book.

CHAPTER 2:

ESSA AL-SALEH

"[Being a leader] comes down to being continually dissatisfied —
not in an angry, irrational way, but in a positive spirit."

Essa Al-Saleh is CEO and board member of Swedish electric-vehicle manufacturer Volta Trucks, an emerging disruptor building an electric truck company that is enabling the transition in commercial vehicles from the fossil fuel ecosystem to one that is safe and sustainable in an urban setting. Previously, he spent more than two decades at Agility Global Integrated Logistics in Baar, Switzerland, where he was appointed president and CEO in 2007. During his time at Agility, he transformed the company from a 300-person, single-country operation into one of the top ten global logistics businesses, operating in over 100 countries, employing more than 18,000 people, and with over $4 billion in revenues.

Having been at the top echelons of management, running multibillion-dollar businesses for over a decade, Essa Al-Saleh has developed a mindset that allows him to be comfortable about being uncomfortable. "It comes down to being continually dissatisfied — not in an angry, irrational way, but in a positive spirit," he explains. "It helps if you have an agile mindset where you are willing to start something, take risks, and iterate in short cycles. As a leader, cultivating a mindset where you're never satisfied [means] you avoid becoming lethargic, which is a sure way to lead you downhill."

Al-Saleh says that one metric that distinguishes a good leader is their propensity to take calculated risks — a trait that is often absent in leaders who believe that they have perfected their game. "Satisfied people are unwilling to entertain new ideas or concepts. While at Agility, I came across the old school-versus-new school debate in risk-taking. I believe neither of them is completely right or wrong. While one needs to embrace new ideas, the other needs to learn from the past. Both parties need to grow and learn to transform and manage change — which brings me back to the ability to be comfortably uncomfortable."

When Al-Saleh took over as the CEO of Agility in 2007 the organization was ripe for change, as it had acquired dozens of companies in quick succession. Al-Saleh explains a concept he abbreviates as "DVP" (which he derived from a leader he has worked with over the years who formulated it based on his personal experience in driving change, including during his time as a partner at McKinsey), which became his guiding mantra to effect change management within Agility.

"D stands for creating a *desire* to change — building the desire for people to change is the first step. V stands for *vision* — you have to show people a vision of the future that they can put their energies into. P stands for *process* — it's about helping your people with the tools and steps to get where you want to take them.

"I believe that the greater the degree of change, the greater its price. This idea has been central to my career. I've always strived to push myself to learn and climb the next levels in my journey. When you have a vision for the future, you're motivated to push yourself out of your comfort zone and do whatever it takes to make it a reality."

BUILDING A BUSINESS BY CHASING POSSIBILITIES AND THINKING AHEAD

To pursue an ambitious path, Al-Saleh contends that leaders must have a tinge of naiveté. "If you aren't naive you won't believe the possibilities, and fear sets in right at the start of your journey. I've got many things right in my journey, but the few wrongs have taught me something valuable. In some of them, we lacked a clear vision for the future, and in others, we set wrong expectations and failed at managing them correctly.

"In most cases, when we started acquiring companies, it was easier to integrate the hardware side of things than people. In some situations, we failed to integrate the people culturally: they didn't understand our values and expectations, and we weren't clear in communicating them. So I think integrating the people's side of a company is the harder part."

With Al-Saleh at the helm, Agility acquired over forty companies in a span of three years — almost one company every month on average. To ensure there was quick integration, Agility put a lot of effort into driving alignment, which included creating clarity about the organization's vision and ensuring people understood the key priorities that would help the company reach its target.

"I focused on empowering and engaging people to make them do what they needed to do. I gave them space to demonstrate their capabilities and learn to iterate from their experiences," Al-Saleh says. "This might sound philosophical, but I tell my people to stop dwelling on their mistakes and focus more on what they can get right. This mentality has worked for us — we learn from our experiences and move on."

Al-Saleh contends that the pace of change is fast, and legacy companies are always playing catch-up. This is especially true of the electric truck business, in which Al-Saleh currently works as the CEO at Volta Trucks, and where he is at the center of the transition to a more sustainable future in transportation.

"In the electric truck business, major tailwinds exist as shareholders demand more sustainable solutions and governments introduce regulations that drive the market. Governments fixing strict road-maps to phasing out diesel vehicles is an inflection point. However, there aren't enough trucks to support current and future demand for electric vehicles. Customers are frustrated due to the lack of volume and capacity. We at Volta are building the capacity to meet the expected demands and opportunities."

RECRUITING THE SUPPLY CHAIN TALENT THAT MATTERS

Unlike many other sectors, supply chains aren't a nine-to-five job. Being pushed into new, high-stress environments is part of being at the forefront of logistics operations, where leaders are expected to take up their responsibilities from the get-go. To ensure processes flow seamlessly, it is critical to pick talent that is unfazed when faced with adversity. "At Agility, I made sure we had motivated people and they knew our strategic plans and capabilities," says Al-Saleh.

Whether he is investing through Agitero or leading an organization like Agility or Volta Trucks, surrounding himself with a great team is critical for Al-Saleh. In all his enterprises, he has sought to nurture and attract talent who had the right skills, values and mindset for building and scaling up the businesses. On the latter note, Al-Saleh points out that "People today are mission-driven and want to under-stand their work's impact on climate change" — a generational shift toward an informed knowledge of and dedication to the principle of sustainability that aligns particularly well with both Volta's business and the supply chain industry in general, given the substantial part it plays in global carbon emissions.

Picking people is a skill that Al-Saleh has cultivated over the years. "I use five dimensions to gauge people when I interview them," he explains. "The first is strategic orientation. I question people's ability to synthesize, simplify, and connect dots to tell a strategic story. The second is their performance management approach. I try to understand how well the person can drive a performance culture and engage with rhythms and routines, while taking accountability and ownership of tough decisions."

The values and character of the individual is the third quality Al-Saleh looks at: "the person could be talented, but I'd have a problem if they are not true to themselves or the values of the company." The fourth revolves around working styles: "are they hard-working, or are they smart-working, or both? I don't want people who only use brute force to achieve results." It is only at the final step that "I look at the skills and expertise they bring along."

MEASURING SUPPLY CHAIN SUCCESS BASED ON OPERATIONAL FLEXIBILITY

An issue that pops up quite often within large organizations is that of information silos: people tend to keep information to themselves, which hampers the seamless transmission of data and knowledge throughout the company. For his part, Al-Saleh reckons that such silo-thinking is default human nature.

"We like to think and focus based on what we can control. This is why the term 'supply chain' is the right phrase. However, companies often operate 'supply silos' that create issues and painful surprises. I believe we need technology and more integrated steps to make the supply chain more integrated," he says.

To that point, Al-Saleh highlights the overarching impact technology has in envisioning streamlined end-to-end supply chains of the future. Driving technology in the supply chain can create solutions with higher impact combined with a stronger team that can better visualize the entire value chain, and thus make more informed decisions.

"I can already see the difference technology has brought in our operations. Thanks to connectivity and improved visibility, our procurement team can work closely with the sales, logistics, and supplier engagement teams. It has made people more aware of their responsibilities and provides them with the necessary information they need at every step of the way."

A lot has changed since the pandemic, Al-Saleh attests. COVID created a tectonic shift within supply chains that woke stakeholders up to the reality of their dependence on systems they didn't realize they were crucially reliant on previously. To take one particularly notable example, the impact of semiconductor chips on auto supply chains vividly illustrated how the lack of one tiny item could bring manufacturing lines around the globe to a standstill.

"Before the pandemic, consumers took the supply chain for granted," Al-Saleh says. "They went to the store and got the items they wanted. They never had to worry about the networks that brought the goods to their destination. It was like breathing for them: the supply chain was involuntary and invisible. But the pandemic changed that significantly."

The fact that supply chain issues are now part of general dinner-table conversation is a massive change in the status quo, and will greatly impact how supply chains evolve going forward. "The disruption brought about by the pandemic led to many businesses ditching the idea of just-in-time inventory, as it doesn't make sense anymore," Al-Saleh says. "At Volta, we're forecasting and making procurement decisions twelve to fifteen months in advance to ensure we have what we need at the right time and place."

INFLUENCING AS A TOOL TO HOLD AN ORGANIZATION TOGETHER

For Al-Saleh, the cardinal trait of a successful leader is to exert a positive influence on the organization and its people. "You have to influence the hearts and minds of people if you want them to agree to your decisions. I use my change management principles to do this. In business strategy, you need some explaining done on why you're doing what you're doing. Taking a philosophical detour can help improve execution."

To illustrate this point, Al-Saleh relates an anecdote from early in his stint at Agility. At that time, before he truly strategized acquisitions, Al-Saleh took a slow, organic approach to build joint ventures with companies. While this was effective, it took a long time to make progress.

"Eventually, I realized acquisitions were faster if I wanted to scale, grow, and achieve the company targets on time," Al-Saleh says. "I committed myself to hire and build the company's M&A team. We made this a top-down decision because we wanted to create impact in a short time. The pace of our acquisitions demanded several important decisions be made at the nick of time, which involved convincing people [to agree with each other] — and I, as the CEO, was everywhere, influencing and persuading my team to make quick progress.

"I remember our acquisition of Geologistics pretty well. It was one of our biggest acquisitions, at half a billion euros. While it wasn't a high-performing company we still decided to go ahead with the merger, as from a strategic point of view we could use it to build a global network that integrates nicely with the rest of our systems." While convincing the shareholders was difficult at first, Al-Saleh's ability to clearly explain and justify the investment elicited a positive response. "It was one of those situations where I used my vision for the future to help the shareholders adapt and adjust. The rationale behind my argument that such a move would yield returns down the line was largely acceptable — and to be honest, I continue to use similar strategies with my investors."

"People who fear making mistakes can't move forward over time. History is witness to the fact that anyone

who does this misses the chance to grow."

That said, mistakes do happen. Al-Saleh recalls an incident in which Agility hired a large communications provider, which ended up costing the company a lot more than anticipated due to a few elements in the contract not aligning with their predetermined expectations. "Everything comes with a consequence. You could lose money in some cases, and your reputation in others. But it's about focusing on recovering, adjusting, and learning from your mistakes.

"The bottom line is that mistakes are unavoidable — be it hiring, acquisitions, or customer onboarding. I try to use the learnings from my past mistakes to formulate future strategies. You need to go through a lot in your career. If the move doesn't make sense, don't do it. But if you decide to go ahead, don't be afraid of making mistakes. People who fear making mistakes can't move forward over time. History is witness to the fact that anyone who does this misses the chance to grow."

Scan the QR code below or visit www.sourcetosold.com to access exclusive bonus content you can use with your teams to further explore the concepts and insights covered in this book.

CHAPTER 3:

KEN ALLEN

"The real sign of success [as a leader] is when the person who comes after you builds on what you've done and makes it even better."

Ken Allen has been with the Deutsche Post DHL group for 35 years in various roles and capacities, and currently serves as the CEO of DHL eCommerce. As global CEO of DHL Express from 2009 to 2018, he helped the company reverse over a decade of poor financial performance and declining market share to become one of the most profitable transportation units in the world. Allen chronicled the story of this turnaround in his book *Radical Simplicity: How Simplicity Transformed a Loss-making Mega Brand into a World-class Performer*.

Since taking over as head of DHL Express in 2008, Ken Allen took the DHL subsidiary from losing over €2.2 billion annually to making an EBIT of roughly €2 billion a decade later. While this balance-sheet turnaround alone testifies to his leadership bona fides, Allen contends that more intangible qualities are just as important to his style of leadership — such as the inspirational songs he frequently belts out during DHL management meetings.

"I think of strategy a bit differently to others in the industry. I believe every strategy revolves around three core principles: motivating people to keep service levels high, creating a loyal customer base, and making money," Allen explains. "I sing inspirational songs during meetings and encourage people to sing along. Songs aren't just to sing: they are a simple and easy way to communicate, and to understand. They help keep our people spirited, create a sense of belonging, and stay connected to a single goal of stopping at nothing for our customers.

"The idea here is for leaders to build their language around things they want to express. It should be something that people can connect to as soon as they hear it. For instance, we came across one of our couriers in South Africa who recited our entire strategy because we'd made it simple to remember and easy to understand."

When people in the network have clear goals and can work as a team, it is reflected in customer retention numbers. "I tell my people that if we give the customer exactly what they want, they will be our best marketing engine and the best route to profitability," Allen says. "If you spend time looking after them, they're much more likely to give you a small premium in return. They also give you a lot of feedback if you're doing it well. All this culminated in the successful business that DHL Express is today."

That said, Allen also advises that when seeking to put together a well-rounded strategy you should take note of the market trends playing out around you. "The '80s was when postal companies looked to transition from documents to parcels. For DHL, this created many run-ins with post offices around the world as we built a global business by moving documents for shipping companies and banks," he recounts.

"I remember predicting this to be a huge move back then, [because] a document can be a piece of paper, but a parcel could be the size of a printer. This required massive increases in infrastructure and better connections to customs authorities, as parcels — unlike documents — were subject to general inspection."

For DHL, this meant thinking about Capex requirements, data needs, customs and security procedures, and considerably detailed parcel screenings. The company had to redesign its pricing and planning procedures to accommodate and afford those changes. "On top of that, the unreliability of belly space in passenger aircraft drove us to build our own fleet of aircraft, as we couldn't afford to depend on them due to our strict transit-time requirements," Allen notes.

Four decades later, with e-commerce now in the picture, Allen says that there is an overwhelming need to transition logistics networks to deliver packages and deliver quickly. "Considering e-commerce requires personal handover of goods in the last mile, it requires a lot more labor and equipment, which inevitably leads to labor and energy inflation. [For this reason], it is critical to put together strategies that help not just with motivating people in the company, but also in ensuring a steady stream of people ready to join the workforce."

THE PEOPLE AND PROCESSES POWERING ORGANIZATIONAL TRANSFORMATION

As a leader, Allen feels strongly that those processes that do not contribute to the organization's success story need to be reshaped. "Transformation is largely about internalizing the cold, hard reality at face value and making decisions that could one day turn out to be genius or lousy. It's heartbreaking work, because you have to make a lot of hard decisions that impact people's lives," he reflects.

Nonetheless, Allen is convinced that the real heroes in an organization are not the leaders who sit at the top of the organizational pyramid, but the ones who grind out growth year in and year out without significant restructuring or laying people off. "These are the people who turn around businesses — the ones who follow through with great business plans," Allen remarks.

"Before I took over as global head of DHL Express, I was the CEO of DHL Express US. When I moved to the US to take up the job, I found us staring at losses that topped $160 million a month. I pulled in an operations guy who I knew could execute better. While I wasn't expecting him to develop a long-term strategy, I wanted someone to keep global operations seamlessly running while we exited certain domestic bases.

Allen explains how the "operations guy" he selected mixed with everyone else with ease, guided people when they were in need, and always knew exactly what he was doing. "I think this was one of those instances where staying with the same company over your career can help, as you can leverage the right people in the right situations," he says.

"In a service industry like ours, the leadership of the frontline people is critical to the business' success. This is something I always keep in mind while choosing my people.

"The experts I call up exhibit simplicity and focus. Contrary to popular belief, 'simple' does not mean 'easy.' Simplifying operations is critical, as it breaks a problem down and makes it easier for people to explain and understand processes — be it the frontline courier or the country manager."

Allen's playbook for building a team involves him asking individuals about the problems they've solved at work. "Hands-on experience is what I seek. Tell me your experiences, like the time you went to a warehouse with boxes stacked up at its gateway and solved the issue by putting a new system in place. I need the details, as merely glossing over points from your CV wouldn't work," he explains.

"This is why hiring at lower levels in the organization is so difficult today. We look for people with integrity who can do a great job with our customers, but most of the time, applicants are not really motivated to be at this job. So building a team is about managing expectations and inspecting what you've got at hand. A strong team should have people with leadership qualities who take the company's values to heart. When you give them more responsibility to show their talent, you'd be surprised at the positive changes they bring to the company."

This is very much the case at DHL Express, Allen attests. "When I left in 2018, the company made €2 billion in profit. My successor, a 30-year Express veteran, doubled that to €4 billion by 2021, and we went from being sixth on the list of best places to work in the world to topping it, reflecting our continuous investment in people.

"This, to me, was my proudest moment. The real sign of success is when the person who comes after you builds on what you've done and makes it even better. Visionary leadership is not just about steering a company while you're at its helm, but making your presence felt even after you've left the scene."

RUNNING AGILE OPERATIONS AS AN ESTABLISHED MARKET INCUMBENT

In recent years, the logistics industry has witnessed a surge in freight SMEs seeking to disrupt the status quo by using technology to provide much-improved service levels, which has made incumbent mega-companies like DHL sit up and take notice. Addressing this development, Allen points to some of the crucial differences between leading a major player like DHL versus a nominally nimbler SME.

"A company like DHL comes with its own set of problems. For instance, we have a disparate set of systems and infrastructure all around the place. One of the first things I did to drive profitability and efficiency was to collapse 2,400 technology applications into 140, and feed them into a system to ensure centralized control. These are issues that SMEs or start-ups will never face."

There's also the need for cybersecurity in a world that's going increasingly digital. "I don't think start-ups worry about cybersecurity the way we do," Allen says. "If you look at cyberattack trends in our industry, major companies like TNT, Maersk, and FedEx have all been compromised. So, we work with systems that prioritize security. While our scale and size are reasons for needing such high cybersecurity, it is also the reason [that we can] afford such systems."

Nevertheless, running agile operations is paramount given that supply chains are now under pressure to adhere to ever-speedier delivery times. Now that the "Amazon Effect" of centering supply chains around the end customer has truly taken hold of the field, placing a premium on the customer's needs is what makes or breaks a company today.

Regarding DHL's response to this new reality, Allen says that "We connect with our top 100 customers to discuss technology solutions. The central idea is to look at the latest technology and figure out how it applies to our industry. We also observe how competitors use it, and if they fare better.

"One such area is robotics. We've scaled our use of robots after looking at our customers. We put the technology through the lens, break down the beneficial elements, and figure out ways to imbibe them into operations. A lot of this involves helping our frontline. Even with robotics, we maintain that it will never replace our people, but only serve to augment their work.

"When you operate a business at a massive scale like DHL, you need to be systematic in moving things forward. Unlike start-ups, we need to test everything we're going to move out thoroughly before rolling it out in several different countries. We can't afford to get carried away by the features. Nonetheless, our entire growth capability has been based on technology since our first inflection point in the '80s, when we moved from documents to parcels."

THE RADICAL SIMPLICITY OF SUPPLY CHAIN LEADERSHIP

"I like making up acronyms," chuckles Allen. "In my book *Radical Simplicity*, I talk about self-reflection and explain SELF as an acronym. 'S' stands for simplicity. My motto is to keep it simple, especially in the international express industry, where everything remains complicated. 'E' is for the execution of all our strategies. I saw empirical evidence from McKinsey that 86 percent of strategies put forward in the banking industry are the same. It's the same for the international express industry, too, be it DHL or FedEx, or UPS.

"'L' is for leadership. [As a leader], people should be happy when you *enter* the room, not when you leave it. Only an expert can lay out the workings of their organization in simple terms for people and can, therefore, lead. That said, experts aren't gods: they're people like you and me, who learn the bottom-to-top elements of a business.

"Finally, 'F' stands for focus. I always believe that anybody with five priorities has no priority. You should only be doing one big thing at a time."

Allen underscores how important it was to practically apply these principles within DHL. The songs he sang during meetings, for example, were one means of keeping things simple — of reminding everyone in the room that they aren't simply functions, numbers or designations, but people working together as a team toward a common goal. (He particularly recalls the camaraderie that was generated by having the room sing genially taunting songs aimed at the competition, such as, "Wanna be a billionaire so frickin' bad / UPS and FedEx will be sad / Want to be on the cover of *Forbes* Magazine / TNT is never to be seen.")

"A lot of such songs came from [working at] the organization," Allen laughs. "It does sound crazy, and it's not for everybody. But such songs work for me, and keep me running hard. And it does seem to have a similar effect on a lot of our people."

Allen believes in the power of a unified leadership under a single voice, which he points to as one of the reasons for DHL Express' success with him as chief executive. "I like to believe there's just one main strategist in the company, and that's me. There's a reason for this — without leaders like the CEO of a division, multiple strategies can be plotted out but none of them will get executed. As the company's head, if I've decided on a strategy, it should seal the deal and people should start working toward that goal. If not, we'll get lost in useless debate, and it will be a collective failure."

> "Like customers, employees are also your best marketing machines: if your employees love working for you they will talk positively about you, and that will inevitably pull in better people who want to be associated with your brand."

To ensure people stay motivated, Allen advocates that management should listen more to the employees' needs. "At DHL, we have an annual employee opinion survey that tells us where we stand as an organization in the eyes of our workers. This is important, as we're a company driven by a purpose — to connect people and improve lives.

"In that regard, we accord our employees as much value as we do our customers. Like customers, employees are also your best marketing machines: if your employees love working for you they will talk positively about you, and that will inevitably pull in better people who want to be associated with your brand. That's precisely how you build a company."

Scan the QR code below or visit www.sourcetosold.com to access exclusive bonus content you can use with your teams to further explore the concepts and insights covered in this book.

CHAPTER 4:

MICHAEL CORBO

"Strategy only works if you have a culture that motivates people ... People will only get you where you want to go if they believe in you — and if they understand not just what, but also why."

Michael Corbo has been the chief supply chain officer of Colgate–Palmolive since 2011, the culmination of a lifelong career with the brand that began in 1982. Prior to his CSCO role he held a number of other senior positions within the company, including vice president of the global oral supply chain (2005–2011) and successive regional VP of manufacturing roles for Central Europe, Asia Pacific, and Latin America.

Having banked forty years at Colgate–Palmolive, Michael Corbo has spanned the equivalent of nearly two generations in his career at the health and hygiene company, which, he attests, has given him unparalleled experience at the heart of the company's supply chain operations. Yet he confesses, "when I graduated from Lafayette College with a degree in engineering, I didn't have a particular inclination toward the supply chain. All I knew was I wasn't meant to be sitting at a desk and designing things as an individual working alone. Operations management and communicating with people were what I liked, and this got me started in the supply chain.

"I joined Colgate right out of college, at our Jersey City manufacturing facility. In the first five years of my career, my focus was on managing people on the factory floor. The best part of being on the floor was that I got to see things from manufacturing down to the warehouse level, and this gave me a feeling of accomplishment. I played a major role in making operations tick by leading the people who made the operations tick."

This resulted in a desire to control how the operations under his watch were run, which, Corbo admits, might have led to him sometimes micromanaging the people who worked under him. "Thankfully, I was lucky to work with senior leaders who reminded me that I needed to stop looking to control everything and start leading instead. They told me my job was to point people in the right direction and lead them toward it."

This advice helped Corbo break free from the need to totally control operations (and people) and, instead, shift his energies to influencing, motivating, leading, and inspiring others in the organization. "Looking back, this was much-needed, and I needed the time and space to develop this leadership expertise. No one can lead 20,000 people around the globe alone, or learn to do so without support. A leader has to be able to motivate and inspire the people they rely on to do the groundwork, and we only learn how to do this over time."

LEADERSHIP TENETS FOR SURVIVING DISRUPTION AND STAYING RELEVANT

"Peter Drucker had rightly said that culture eats strategy for breakfast. Strategy only works if you have a culture that motivates people and helps them understand their purpose and how that fits with their company's purpose — which, at Colgate, is to imagine a healthier future for all people, their pets, and our planet," Corbo says. "People will only get you where you want to go if they believe in you — and if they understand not just what, but also why."

Leveraging his four decades of leadership experience and drawing on the lessons he's learned from steering Colgate–Palmolive through other challenging situations over the years (such as when Argentina devalued its currency in 2002, which required an aggressive ramping up of local production), Corbo has consistently prioritized flexibility in Colgate's response to the pandemic, adjusting organizational strategy according to the demands of the (often volatile) situation. "Right now, companies are forced to think of ways to strike a balance between sourcing regionally and globally. In that regard, I frequently revisit my previous experiences, analyzing the pros and cons of the measures we took when we had our back to the wall," he says.

Corbo contends that to be objective in making decisions during such challenging times, it is critical to look at situations from a balanced point of view after carefully weighing all different perspectives. "For instance, while being mindful of our carbon footprint was not high on the list of our priorities in the past, it absolutely is today — and is critical to our future as we work to reimagine a healthier future for all people, their pets and our planet. We've also learned important lessons in just the past couple of years. Increasingly, I find we are leveraging knowledge as much as equipment, and that will result in more resilience, agility, and flexibility in supply chains than in the times pre-COVID."

Part and parcel of this knowledge-gathering is making sure to stay current on what is happening in supply chains elsewhere. "To be informed, it helps to expand connections that go beyond the organization," Corbo says. "I've created a network of peers that respect and trust each other. Once or twice a year, we get in touch over conferences and calls. It's been helpful."

Yet while such discussions are constructive in suggesting potentially beneficial alternative methods of working, actually implementing changes within supply chain operations is a long-term project. "They do not materialize overnight, and you can't just scrap what you were doing all along and do something else," acknowledges Corbo. "Evolution and growth demand progressive changes over time. You need to spark curiosity and encourage experiments. If I find an interesting trend, I talk to my team about it, and I also get pitches from them sometimes. If it looks interesting, we do a deep pilot dive, check its applicability, and study its use cases."

Nonetheless, a disruption on the scale of the pandemic necessitated that even the most careful and rigorous organizations respond swiftly and decisively, implementing emergency-response measures absent trial-ballooning. "Previously, disruptions were events that happened and cleared up within three to six months. That's not what we saw with COVID-19," Corbo says. "Fires were burning in different parts of the world simultaneously. Benchmarking data wasn't enough, as situations kept changing rapidly. This is when you realize there's no one-stop solution to logistics. You have to become agile and take things as they come."

While such scenarios are taxing, Corbo seems to enjoy the firefighting in some respects — which, he suggests, is one of the integral qualities of being a great supply chain leader. "Of course, over the span of forty years there have been moments where I've contemplated going in a different direction. I've stayed here because Colgate keeps presenting new challenges and giving me opportunities to innovate and grow, whether as a plant manager or now as the leader of 20,000 people.

"The routine isn't the exciting part of the job. I would rather be an agent of change and try something new than be a caretaker. If ever I felt my work getting monotonous, I'd look to myself to find new challenges. That mindset and approach have led me to where I am today."

DEVELOPING FUTURE LEADERS IN SUPPLY CHAIN

Even though Colgate boasts a legacy spanning over 200 years and is a brand ubiquitous in homes across the world, Corbo contends that one of the keys to the company's endurance is its openness to innovation, new ideas, and change. "We tell our new recruits that while we want to teach them, we also want to learn from them. They come with a lot of the latest skills and competencies that we need, and we help them understand how to apply those abilities to growing the business.

"Look no further than the relationship we have with our interns. Our interns work on real projects and are empowered to think critically to help us find solutions. We're excited to see what that can do for us, and we trust them to get the job done. One college intern once helped save roughly a million dollars over her eight-week summer internship.

"We also understand interns don't necessarily have a ton of experience. We give them opportunities to learn and make sure they have the support they need to rise to the challenge of working at an industry-leading operation."

Among the salaried ranks, meanwhile, Colgate seeks to provide opportunities for professional growth at all levels and foster diversity in all sectors. The supply chain operation is keen on advancing women and people of color into leadership positions, and leverages a robust talent management system to ensure the company is considering a diverse slate of candidates.

"I'm especially proud of how much progress we've made when it comes to bringing women into the supply chain and advancing their professional development," Corbo says. "It begins with recruiting, which wasn't always easy, since engineering programs historically were more male-dominated. This is why Colgate actively supports opportunities for women in STEM, so that we may continue to promote gender diversity within the supply chain."

Corbo is committed to creating a workplace environment where everyone feels like they belong, and are empowered to be their authentic selves. "In any workplace, and especially in a shop-floor environment, it's important to ensure people feel confident speaking up and also feel heard when they raise their voice. When we resolve those issues together, we become a better organization."

FOSTERING RELATIONSHIPS ON ALL RUNGS OF THE ORGANIZATIONAL LADDER

Corbo stresses to his teams that the supply chain does not function within a silo, but is integral to and intermixed with the entire operation. As such, the company ensures that supply chain interns and employees alike witness the workings of all major segments within the business — including sales, marketing, and finance — so that they can understand how they all translate into product supply. "Comprehensive exposure to the business can help them understand how sales promotions, marketing campaigns, and cost operations are linked to the supply chain, even more so within the scope of sustainability, diversity, and inclusion," Corbo says.

> "We could be developing a future company CEO within the supply chain, but this can only happen if supply chain people have access to diverse experiences."

In addition to this cross-departmental exposure, Corbo avers that there is a concerted effort within Colgate to create and encourage meaningful interactions vertically as well — a novel policy, given that employees who focus on supply chain management have traditionally not intermixed with the company's other business areas. "Today, it's clear that it's better to have people exposed to all segments within the company. Senior leaders at Colgate recognize that we could be developing a future company CEO within the supply chain. This can only happen if supply chain people have access to diverse experiences."

Moreover, experience in supply chain is increasingly being seen as essential training for future leaders, as it provides such a rich understanding of how the business fundamentally works. "Since the pandemic, there's been a definite change in how the top management looks at supply chain professionals," notes Corbo. "There's growing recognition for the vast business acumen the company generates from its supply chain division."

BUILDING OPERATIONAL RESILIENCY IN A STATE OF SUPPLY CHAIN FLUX

Now more than ever there are new opportunities to implement innovative technology within the supply chain, and Corbo's team is tasked with integrating these solutions in a way that adds the most value. "The present-day data correction and data ingestion techniques are very sophisticated compared to what they were in the past. Data analysis was backward-looking in the past, but it's become more predictive now. Today, you can use advanced tools to analyze a large amount of data in a short time."

At the same time, truly intelligent leadership entails leveraging experience to identify the blind spots in certain process adoptions. "I take everything with a grain of salt," Corbo says. "You've got to be careful, because sometimes these new solutions can be boosted by marketing shine and not necessarily backed up by reality. As a leader, you need to consider limitations every time and explain to your subordinates how just because something works in a particular scenario, it does not mean it will work for us, too."

For Corbo, the supply chain is a real, tangible entity, not just a set of numbers and data analytics. "In a company like Colgate that produces the majority of what it sells, you see how manufacturing plants react to demand spikes. It's almost like a living thing. Only when you see how data is integral to real-time results will you feel empowered to use insights to make the right choices. Supply chain management helps you do that."

Two or three decades ago, Corbo explains, supply chain operations were chiefly focused on reducing costs; today, it is less about the number of assets deployed and more about properly connecting the dots in order to promptly and efficiently respond to upticks in demand. "In today's times, you can't just be a cost-base operation and succeed. The best cost might not always yield the best growth. So you have to think beyond cost parameters and reckon with agility, resiliency, and sustainability.

"That doesn't mean we forget the fundamentals, but it can't all be bottom-line-driven. COVID-19 showed us that, as it taught us how to be resilient and adapt to change. The scenarios were not perfect, but by navigating the challenges with an eye toward flexibility, we could still drive growth. Some of those older KPIs made sense when things got a bit stable, while others we continue to update and re-evaluate in real time."

OPTIMIZING TO STAY AHEAD OF THE CURVE

As the pandemic wanes and consumer behavior and retail trends continue to change, Corbo intends to seize new opportunities to optimize the supply chain and position Colgate for continued leadership. "We are standing at the crossroads of change in the retail market, which will inevitably impact the future of the supply chain. Colgate is seriously considering the possibility of stacking — of having a plant within a plant, or a supply chain within a supply chain. The aim is to move toward a highly efficient and flexible model. Handling the cost structures may be challenging, but the intended outcomes balance growth, efficiency, and flexibility, which is the need of the hour."

Corbo opines that 2021 was a monumental year for retail, as extreme surges in demand forced supply chains to evolve. "And evolve fast, it did. We had to make fast decisions. In the end, prioritizing growth and deciding to figure out costs later was what got us through."

To Corbo, the pandemic is an inflection point. "It has created numerous challenges for organizations and illustrated just how essential a role the supply chain plays, not just within a company but also within the lives of consumers. The need to build resiliency within supply chains is greater than ever so that we can continue to navigate new challenges that arise and come out stronger.

"Working in a truly global organization like Colgate–Palmolive, which has a presence in more than 200 countries and territories, it is easy to see that the supply chain is more than just logistics or manufacturing. Understanding it demands mastering its end-to-end operations, all the way down several tiers of suppliers to the end consumer. In the end, it's clear that the supply chain can make or break a great company."

Scan the QR code below or visit www.sourcetosold.com to access exclusive bonus content you can use with your teams to further explore the concepts and insights covered in this book.

CHAPTER 5:

ACHIM DÜNNWALD

"Visibility and authenticity are crucial to being a leader."

Achim Dünnwald is chief operating officer at GLS, and an adviser and VC investor. Prior to that he was chief operating officer at Royal Mail in the UK, and previously at Deutsche Post DHL (DPDHL) Group in Bonn, Germany, where he served as CEO of mail communication and international mail and, subsequently, as CEO of DHL Parcel. Before joining DPDHL in 2013, he spent twelve years at McKinsey & Company as a partner, a member of the German management board, and as head of the global post, express and parcel industry group.

While Achim Dünnwald has made his presence felt in the highest levels of supply chain leadership, his first foray into the industry was largely incidental. "I had no background in logistics when I took my first project in Bonn with the Deutsche Post in 2000, working for McKinsey as a consultant," he says. "I had an MBA from UC Berkeley, and before moving to the US I had been working for a member of the German parliament."

However, "Logistics drove me the most," he recalls. "Through McKinsey, I was associated with Deutsche Post and DHL for a long time, along with other companies in the industry. I learned a lot from the people I worked with, both clients and colleagues, so I felt motivated to stick around. I tested the waters in a few other industries, with projects in the high-tech and automotive industries. But ultimately, it was the people in logistics that clicked with me, along with a growing level of industry expertise and network."

In 2012, after spending more than a decade in consulting, Dünnwald was asked by his long-term client Jürgen Gerdes, who was at that time a board member at DPDHL, to join the company as CEO of one of its postal businesses. While it was not an easy decision to leave McKinsey, Dünnwald realized that leading the letters business for Deutsche Post was too good an opportunity to pass up. "How often do you have a board member of a global logistics company offer you the chance to leave your mark on a very large business that is going through a major transformation?"

THE VIBRANCY OF SUPPLY CHAIN LEADERSHIP

"There were a lot of new activities to undertake and skills to learn in the transition into a senior executive position," remembers Dünnwald. "Three areas stood out: one, operating in a more rigid corporate structure with a host of topics and decisions to be taken daily, rather than a project-based environment and small teams of clients and consultants working on focused topics. Two, working with a large, geographically dispersed workforce where shared goals, motivation, and a good working relationship with the trade union are key — but not always a given. And three, contributing input and results to the rhythm of quarterly financial reporting when working in a publicly listed company."

Six years later, when he accepted the role of chief operating officer at another major European postal company, Royal Mail, Dünnwald gained even deeper insights into what it took to lead such a large workforce.

"Aligning the organization to a shared purpose and providing a narrative around the elements of our transformation at Royal Mail became a key objective of my role. That purpose and narrative

— in other words, the why and what — was to ensure we were all broadly marching the same way. I was vocal and used a variety of communication channels to relay my message across a geographically dispersed organization. In the light of this experience, [I've found that] visibility and authenticity are crucial to being a leader."

At the end of the day, Dünnwald stresses, leadership's words and actions influence the lives and livelihoods of thousands of employees and their families. "Make no mistake, the burden of the company doesn't rest on any one [person]'s shoulders alone — it is always a team effort. But a major element of my role was to tell a purpose-driven story and set the company's journey onto the right path."

TEAM-BUILDING: PUTTING THE RIGHT PEOPLE IN THE RIGHT PLACE

Successful organizations have one common denominator: teams with complementary skills where every member knows their role and can execute it to the best of their abilities. When Dünnwald first joined Deutsche Post, he worked with a team that had operated under stable conditions for quite some time — namely, in a declining letter market, not being at the top of the priority list, and with no explicit change or people-development agenda.

"The team had a lot of expertise, but there wasn't much momentum. To bring them together, I focused on building medium- to longer-term plans, and on what and how people could contribute to implementing the plan given their skills. The underlying idea was to match tasks with skills and experiences across the team. I also considered how people complement each other. This included reshuffling and bringing in talent from [both] the wider company and externally."

When he became CEO of DHL Parcel in Europe some years later, Dünnwald faced a similar task, but in a very different environment.

Here, he needed to work with teams across many European countries, all while the business was growing at breakneck speed. "When I took over the role, DHL Parcel Europe's revenue was about €800 million, and when I left, it had tripled to nearly €2.5 billion," he recalls. "We executed this massive growth with a team of country managers and a small central team in Bonn. We aligned with the same vision and purpose, and focused on a set of core KPIs across all functions."

"Not everything can be, or should be, centrally coordinated. There needs to be a common purpose and clarity in measuring success. It then comes down to unleashing the team's energy to enact the strategy and deliver the results."

Scaling up an organization required teams from different backgrounds to get their heads together and think as a single, cohesive unit. Dünnwald organized leadership meetings at least once a quarter to build camaraderie, strengthen the social element and encourage networking. "Not everything can be, or should be, centrally coordinated. There needs to be a common purpose and clarity in measuring success. It then comes down to unleashing the team's energy to enact the strategy and deliver the results."

THE MANY COMPLEXITIES OF LEADING LOGISTICS OPERATIONS

"I found there were notable differences in the core activities of my roles as a COO and a CEO," observes Dünnwald. "As a CEO leading letter and parcel businesses at Deutsche Post DHL, I spend most of my time setting direction by talking to customers and colleagues and analyzing market demands. As a COO at Royal Mail, it was paramount to engage meaningfully with our frontline and work with unions as partners. Core KPIs are monitored daily — mostly safety-, quality-, and cost-related. Given the size of the organization and the cost of running the operations, getting the metrics wrong even to a small degree can cause major upheaval for employees, customers, or the company finances."

Over the years, Dünnwald has seen a shift in the factors that dominate his work, as issues like e-commerce-driven parcel growth, digitalization, and sustainability have now become pre-eminent among his concerns. In the last decade, Dünnwald found that he was spending more and more time managing e-commerce-driven growth rather than focusing on letter decline, a trend that only accelerated with the COVID-19 pandemic. Building sorting capacity (including significant Capex investments) and finding a workforce with the needed skill sets in an increasingly labor-constrained market are two of the primary challenges that have arisen from this new reality.

Regarding his experience at Royal Mail, Dünnwald highlights the pivot that had to be made from a letter-oriented to a parcel-oriented business. "While the design and implementation of this transformation have been my assigned role all along, the pandemic has definitely accelerated the timeline," he says. "It has increased the opportunity for financial growth by bringing the future forward by three to four years."

In 2019, when Dünnwald was hired by Royal Mail's then-CEO Rico Back (also the founder of the European parcel player GLS) as chief strategy and transformation officer, it was clear that expanding parcel-processing capacity was a key pillar to support the strategy and the anticipated 5%+ annual parcel growth. "However, during the peak season [of] 2020, year-over-year parcel growth was more than 50 percent. With parcels being bigger and heavier than letters, the overall processed volume this translated to was tremendous. As a company, transforming the ways of working to accommodate this increase was an impressive feat."

And yet, the company continues to face pressure from mounting volume. "Of course, it would have been better or at least easier if we had had three more years to keep up with the pace, but it is what it is," Dünnwald says. "The main themes have remained the same, but it now needs to happen much more quickly. And there is a need to be a bit more resourceful and creative in addressing the bottlenecks."

THE PERKS OF BEING IN SUPPLY CHAIN MANAGEMENT

"With more than 20 years in the industry, it can feel like a small world and a bit like a family," Dünnwald says when asked about some of the things he values the most about working in his field. "The advisory work I do is a lot about leveraging this network. For instance, my engagement with Seven Senders, a leading delivery platform based in Germany, started when a private equity fund called Digital Plus, founded by former McKinsey partners, looked at them as an investment opportunity. It's fair to say that the connections in the industry help keep a tab on what's happening in multiple spaces and put pieces of the puzzle together."

This also helps with staying current and curious, Dünnwald points out. "Talking to people in my network is of great use. So are conferences and platforms like LinkedIn, which is a good source of information and a place to feel the pulse of my network. It's on platforms like that where you see personal takes on what you read in the trade press, [or in] online or offline press articles."

There are several reasons why supply chains continue to fascinate Dünnwald. "For one, I firmly believe postal companies serve a major purpose in society, which motivates me. When I had just started with Deutsche Post, there was a state election in Bremen, the smallest state in Germany. The person responsible for organizing the election was constantly in touch with us, and found it interesting how the mail could pull the posted votes and get the count in until the very last minute."

In response, with the help of his colleagues in Bremen, Dünnwald helped organize a few extra runs around pillar boxes on election day. While they only ended up collecting a few hundred more votes, the election organizer wrote to Dünnwald post-election praising Deutsche Post's role in supporting democracy. "While they might sound like big words, that's essentially what we were doing, which made me incredibly proud."

The spirit of supply chains lies in how they always strive to be faster, innovative, and competitive, explains Dünnwald. "It may look like the tech disruptors drive this change, but there's so much more going on at the intrinsic level. Innovations get introduced every day to support decarbonization, organize out-of-home deliveries, and increase customer convenience. This thrill of improving speed, transparency, and flexibility to elevate customer experience [is what] keeps me on my feet.

"Lastly, it's the scale and impact of what I do. One in every 200 employees nationwide works for the two large postal companies I have worked for. If you include their dependents in the UK, this works out to be around 300,000 people whose livelihood depends on us making the right decisions. That puts a lot of responsibility on my shoulders. Working with such a large organization, you know you can have an impact, and that's motivation enough."

Scan the QR code below or visit www.sourcetosold.com to access exclusive bonus content you can use with your teams to further explore the concepts and insights covered in this book.

CHAPTER 6:

BONNIE FETCH

"That's the essence of running a business — challenging the status quo and daring to innovate."

Bonnie Fetch is the vice president and head of global supply chain at Cummins Inc., an American multinational corporation of complementary business units that design, engineer, manufacture, distribute, and service engines and related technologies, including fuel systems, controls, air handling, filtration, emission solutions, and electrical power generation systems. She arrived at Cummins in 2018 from construction equipment giant Caterpillar, where she held a range of positions in logistics, manufacturing, product design, human resources, organizational development and business leadership over the course of 20 years.

Like many other supply chain veterans interviewed for this book, Bonnie Fetch began her career in a completely different industry. In Fetch's case it was the hospitality sector, where she started off in the 1980s by running a restaurant, and then a small travel agency at the beginning of the '90s. "And then the World Wide Web happened, enabling people to book their own travel, effectively sinking my business. This was my first exposure to disruption — something I've grown accustomed to over the course of my career," she recalls.

After the closure of her travel agency Fetch took on temp work with a local staffing company, through which she worked in a logistics company as an inventory control analyst until going off on maternity leave with no expectations to go back to work for a while.

"I had planned to try being a stay-at-home mom," Fetch remembers. "I knew I had the work cut out because it wouldn't be easy for someone like me, who had worked since I was thirteen. So when Caterpillar called me six months later with an offer to fill a new role, I gave it serious consideration." After discussing the options with her husband, Fetch decided it would do a world of good for her mental health if she had a role outside of the house as well. "I had an early morning shift, and planned to come home by 1 p.m.," Fetch recalls. "This was in the mid-'90s, when flexible working arrangements weren't so popular, but I was determined to make it work." She evidently succeeded in that goal, as within a year of starting at Caterpillar she was promoted to supervisor of the inventory control group. Fetch hasn't looked back since.

COMING FULL CIRCLE WITHIN HUMAN RESOURCE MANAGEMENT

Soon after Fetch took on the supervisor role at Caterpillar, her boss pushed her to take over warehouse operations — an area she had no knowledge of at the time. "While I believed he wanted to punish me by putting me in a position where I had no experience, he was actually thinking of rewarding me," Fetch says. "What seemed like torture turned out to be a huge learning opportunity. I ran warehouse operations with a diverse workforce involved in various activities such as unloading trucks, sorting parts, and sending them to the destined locations."

This was where Fetch got her first taste of HR. "I realized my colleagues would do anything for me if I treated them right. After observing how good I was with people, I was offered an HR role. I think part of the reason was that the management knew I had the potential to grow, and women mostly grew in areas like HR in this industrial company."

This certainly held true in Fetch's case. "I excelled in HR. I undertook a couple of successful labor negotiations. I also led miscellaneous functions that didn't fit into anyone's bucket, such as security, accounting, and inventory control. I reached a point where I had grown at the location to the highest point I would go, so I decided I was ready for more and left the company."

After leaving Caterpillar at the beginning of 2001, Fetch took up a role as HR director at a restaurant chain. "I loved being in HR, but I always thought of myself as someone who could take HR into a business role and not the other way around," she says. "I travelled a lot for work, and was rarely home for dinner and infrequently home for holidays." Meanwhile, Caterpillar was still interested. "They called me in the middle of a long trip, asking me if I'd be interested in helming HR shared services. I was weary from all the travelling, and this sounded like a good opportunity, so I took it."

Upon rejoining Caterpillar in 2004, Fetch was determined to avoid being pushed into a corner where she couldn't grow. "But that wasn't the case [this time]. I had good exposure in my role as the senior HR leader. Since my vice president knew I had business experience, he asked me to take on strategy in addition to HR. And when I told him I would not necessarily restrict myself but would expand my role to running a business, he put me through career development discussions with six of his vice president peers. Interestingly, only one of those six was female."

After talking to five male VPs, who were all pleasant enough but not encouraging at all with regard to her career aspirations, Fetch says that it was a welcome contrast to hear from the sole female VP at the company. "She told me to trust myself. She also told me that while the other leaders I spoke to weren't very encouraging, it would only take one successful opportunity in a manufacturing role to gain credibility and they would all forget that I didn't come from a background in industry after that.

"I decided to believe her, as she was pretty successful: she had moved from marketing to the core business, and was only our second female VP ever in the company."

These encounters, as well as her subsequent interactions with people from other firms around the industry, made Fetch acutely aware of how few women were progressing to senior leadership. "Based on my discussions with people from the industry, and men in particular, it is evident that awareness of the problem is an opportunity for women, as many men seemed surprised by the gross underrepresentation of women," she says. "Once aware, many men also genuinely want to help." This led Fetch to write a book on the subject, (Un) skirting the Issues: A Guide for the Well-intentioned Man in Today's Workplace, specifically to inform and inspire that broader group of potential male allies to actively engage in the desired change.

KEEPING A BUSINESS GOING THROUGH RECESSIONS AND DOWNTURNS

As Fetch expressed at the beginning of this chapter, she is no stranger to disruption, and she got another taste of it when she moved to England to take up the reins of Caterpillar's transmission business in her new role as managing director. "This was in July '08, just two weeks before the financial world started collapsing. In Europe, I felt the tremors of change first. At that time I was the only one on my boss' team stationed outside of the US, and thus was uniquely positioned to clearly see the intensity of the problem we were about to experience."

In these difficult times, Fetch's experience managing complex situations and her ability to deal with people came in handy. Over the course of several months she entered redundancy negotiations twice, discussing short work weeks and more, in a desperate attempt to keep Caterpillar's $400 million transmission business afloat. "At our lowest, 75 percent of our business had disappeared," remembers

Fetch. "However, I was far from giving up. We laid out a new product development strategy and outsourced some of our component manufacturing. We started a new plant in India, and restructured the entire business amid the downturn."

In 2010, just when Caterpillar's order book was recovering, Fetch was asked to move back to the US to take on the role of chief learning officer, with a mandate to oversee leadership development and workplace culture. "We had a CEO transition at the time, and he wanted me to work closely with him. I tried hard to convince the management that, having spent the last few years in Europe trying to help the business survive, I wanted to see the consequences of my decisions when everything was turning back up. But it was not to be, so I headed back to the US."

Although Fetch accepted the new position, she continued to argue her case that she should be a leader beyond the HR fold. Her self-advocacy resulted in her being appointed general manager and entrusted with leading a $6 billion business that comprised the design, product management, manufacturing and procurement of all common components across Caterpillar's product suite.

"While I knew manufacturing and product design, this was still a new product portfolio," Fetch recalls. "Yet, I went into this role much more confidently than the previous ones. But almost immediately after I took it up, we had another downturn in the business that was partly self-induced."

In the components business, it pays to be vigilant when inventory levels are high as this exposes the company to excesses, especially if plants and dealers begin to cut orders. This very scenario was enacted soon after Fetch took over Caterpillar's components business, as the company suffered a 65 percent reduction in order volume.

Well-schooled in crisis management by this point, Fetch applied a calmly analytical lens to the situation. "Once again, I looked at our manufacturing capacity and what we should be making versus buying. We needed to deliver value to our customers, but we needed to do it at the cost structure we aimed for. Our division introduced a global leader profile process where we used our vision and our competitive analysis to plan ways to unleash the organization and innovate and work toward our big goals."

Under Fetch's leadership the unit saw its best safety, quality and financial performance, getting her accolades from the top management. "They told me that they'd never seen anyone come into a role and pick the business operations up so intuitively. Frankly, I could make this work because I spent considerable time with my people and trusted them in getting the work done. I listened to them and asked questions. The more comfortable I got with my team and the business, the more I challenged them to innovate and think differently. I think that's the essence of running a business — challenging the status quo and daring to innovate."

THE CHALLENGES (AND PERKS) OF LEADING SUPPLY CHAIN OPERATIONS

One of the characteristics of good leadership is being a voracious learner, which Fetch considers to be one of her top five strengths. "Curiosity has been the centerpiece of my life. I'm curious about how things work, and I use that knowledge to drive my actions," she states. "My willingness to take risks and delve into the unknown has led me to situations where I could have failed terribly. But I've always found merit in persisting and persevering and this could be a key reason why I've been able to maneuver a strange career path to reach where I am today."

Where Fetch is today is Cummins Inc., which she joined in 2018 after being attracted by the company's strong vision and clear focus on diversity and inclusion. "Supply chain operations can make or break the company, and as the chief supply chain officer (CSCO) I enjoy being in that position. I get to see the full view of the company and how we operate. It's exhilarating to be on the team formulating important policies, making critical decisions on what is being produced and where, and deciding the culture propagating within the company."

Aside from being accountable for a substantial portion of the company's employees, the CSCO also has an overview of spending and the revenue brought into the organization. "You never have a dull moment," Fetch says. "You're always juggling business leadership and managing a significant amount of profitability for the company. There's also the implicit trust you build with your colleagues, and they know you're with them in the company's journey through significant transitions. Personally, I love being part of complex supply chain problem-solving. It allows me to question my work every day."

While the importance of the supply chain is not lost within organizations now, it was not quite the same when Fetch first began her career in the field. "When I was in Europe, Caterpillar's supply chain wasn't a discrete function. We had logistics and manufacturing departments, but nothing was specifically under the supply chain function. Since then I've been trying to set up the supply chain function wherever I go, as it's the glue that holds the company together.

"I think the supply chain is a great place to work, as it cuts across the entire business and is the linchpin holding different segments of an organization together. If you are a problem-solver and like to be where the action is, supply chain provides plenty of opportunity for creative problem-solving — and [it's] rewarding too, thanks to its obvious importance to any company."

The potential for creative problem-solving within supply chain is enhanced as the whole world moves further toward digitalization, which allows for greater visibility, building resilience, and planning for the unforeseen crises that Fetch contends will inevitably strike

— like with COVID-19. "One year of experience in the supply chain during this time is equivalent to ten years, as there was always something happening with the chaos that was reverberating across the world," she says.

> "Diversity is a key enabler to solving some of the problems in this industry."

The disruptions wrought by the pandemic brought the crucial role of the supply chain to general public consciousness, as well as its vulnerability. "All this demands more creativity in the industry, [and] younger generations have plenty to offer," declares Fetch. "It pays to understand that the supply chain significantly impacts every area within the company, be it planning, forecasting, producing, delivering, or procuring.

"As a supply chain manager, you can work across the globe, as every company needs people who can make sense of the supply chain. Diversity is a key enabler to solving some of the problems in this industry: I had no background in the supply chain, and yet I've managed to come this far.

"When I look back, I realize that the supply chain wasn't something I had studied at school. It just happened to me. My bit in this equation was to ensure people knew me as someone who could go in and fix complex problems. I let the world know that I was willing to take risks and grow. That, maybe, is the most important advice I could give someone looking to jumpstart a career in supply chain."

Scan the QR code below or visit www.sourcetosold.com to access exclusive bonus content you can use with your teams to further explore the concepts and insights covered in this book.

CHAPTER 7:

DEEPAK GARG

"A [supply chain leader] needs to have skill
sets matching the level of the CEO's."

Deepak Garg is the founder and CEO of Rivigo, which has become the largest and fastest-growing technology-enabled logistics company in India since it was launched in 2018. Prior to starting Rivigo, Garg was an associate partner with McKinsey & Company from 2006 to 2014, where he accrued extensive experience working on complex supply chain issues with major clients across India, Australia and Africa.

Before Deepak Garg founded Rivigo, which today is one of India's most prominent tech start-ups, he spent nine years at McKinsey working in and observing different sectors within the country. Garg's eventual foray into the trucking market came from him connecting the dots between the long-standing issue of the country's dearth of truckers and the critical role that drivers play in moving the national economy.

"The projects I worked on at McKinsey exposed me to trucking problems in India. It surprised me that driver unavailability was a core problem in the industry, even when India had a sizable population that was unemployed," Garg says. "I could not fathom why people wouldn't want to be a truck driver, as they typically earn more than a daily-wager. I realized it was not that simple — the life of a truck driver was one of great hardship. It was something that not many would be willing to sign on for, as it involved them being away from their family for weeks, sleeping uncomfortably in their truck cab, and eating unhealthy food along the way."

While the logistics spend as a percentage of GDP at that time hovered at around 8 percent in developed economies across North America and Europe, India was spending close to 14 percent of its GDP on logistics, with 70 percent of that going toward the trucking sector. It was here that Garg found his calling. "I have a strong conviction that India has the potential to be a superpower in my lifetime. Given these statistics, I decided to bet the next three decades of my life on the trucking industry, as I saw a huge efficiency gap in logistics that needed to be filled," he recalls.

"Customers weren't getting their goods on time, fleet owners weren't making money, and truck drivers weren't living a dignified life. I thought of ways to run trucks more efficiently, because the more efficient they are, the better the transit time and more reliable the customer service. A single, effective solution in the trucking industry could solve all three problems and contribute to 10 percent of India's GDP, which is huge."

For Garg, Rivigo's business model helped tick all these boxes. By harnessing technology to solve a critical macroeconomic problem, the company directly impacts people's lives while simultaneously building a profitable business.

BUILDING A LEADERSHIP PERSONA, ONE STEP AT A TIME

"I've always wanted to run a business," says Garg, whose family background was in trade. "So it was of little surprise to people around me when they knew that my immediate goal after joining McKinsey in 2006 was to quit the company as soon as possible and start my own business. But what I thought would take me two years to achieve actually took nine."

Garg spent his years at McKinsey searching for opportunities across projects, dreaming of disruptive ideas that could help him build India's next big start-up. "If I were involved in insurance work, next to the project I'd look at ways to build a digital insurance broker-age company. When working with a power plant, I put together a fancy business plan in my spare time about creating non-polluting bricks with fly ash. The projects didn't occupy me as much as the idea of what I could create from them. I was so passionate that I'd sometimes spend weekends working on my ideas."

Eventually, Garg realized that bringing such ideas to life would require strong connections within the industry. Accordingly, he set about building relationships with CEOs and senior leadership he encountered through his work at McKinsey. "While I enjoyed this journey, something stopped me from quitting and going ahead with one of my ideas," remarks Garg. "Finally, in 2014, one of my advisers told me that if I didn't leave sight of the shore, I'd never sail the high seas. If I had to do that, I'd have to be confident enough to leave. [So] I just did that, experiencing true liberation and restoring confidence in myself."

Confidence is something that Garg has always had in large reserves. Once, while he was attending a week-long leadership coaching program at one of McKinsey's capability centers, he was asked to write a letter to his future self, describing where he saw himself five years down the line. Garg wrote about how he would be running a $100-million revenue company, and posted the letter to his address back in Delhi.

"I recently came across the letter, and was shocked to see that everything I wrote had happened. I was running a services company with roughly the same value I had projected," he says, adding with a smile: "I couldn't help but think — where would I be if I had put one more zero on that revenue number?"

Garg says that this power of visualization has helped shape who he is today. "I was a shy, introverted kid growing up, but my stint in McKinsey changed me into a confident, self-assured individual. It strengthened my resolve to hold my own in front of CEOs, at board meetings, and while answering to my investors. Growth is a long process, and I work to improve myself every day."

DISSECTING THE HUMAN QUOTIENT OF A FAST-GROWING COMPANY

"To have great leadership is to have an uncanny ability to build a great team," Garg says. "I had a chance to talk with Narendra Modi, India's prime minister, about leadership, and he equated it with team-building. Another element of leadership is pushing your team to be the best versions of themselves. I believe every person fundamentally has infinite potential and capability. It's up to the leader to create an environment to explore that.

"Spiritually speaking, we like to call Rivigo a 'hero's hermitage.' It's a place where leaders come and become the best versions of themselves. So, I prioritize investing a lot of my time in developing leaders. I've made conscious efforts to ensure I run a company where people take on newer challenges and grow well.

"I take pride in the fact that many Indian supply chain leaders have been a part of Rivigo in some way. For instance, the head of Amazon Prime India is an ex-Rivigo. One of my earliest hires was the CEO of a B2C start-up that took the country by storm through its ten-minute delivery model."

"I believe every person fundamentally has infinite potential and capability. It's up to the leader to create an environment to explore that."

Garg explains how Rivigo created a set of eight principles for leadership in the company that set the guidelines for hiring, talent administration, and partner evaluation. These principles are "ownership," "hire and develop," "deep-dive," "think big," "1 percent improvement a day," "respectfully disagree and commit," "cost leadership," and "say/do = 100 percent."

Garg proudly points out the courage Rivigo showed as a young start-up in hiring people and investing in them, even when it is perfectly normal in the current work environment for people to hop companies. "While people become their best version [of themselves], it might so happen that their interests lie elsewhere and not at Rivigo. But I feel that [by investing in them] we hold onto only those people who really want to stay, and that helps us as a company and them as individuals."

Rivigo also runs a strong alumnus connect program that helps it stay in touch with its people. Garg explains that it was vital to keep the door open for people who want to come back at some point in their careers. "Employment is no longer a lifelong affiliation. Today's employment contracts aren't as binding as a few decades ago. I believe the talent of today will keep coming and leaving. Many who've left us to explore growth opportunities have returned to work with us. Surprisingly, 70 percent of our alumni have expressed an interest in joining us again. Investing in people's growth and keeping in touch with them has helped us a lot in the long term."

Even people leaving had something to offer Rivigo. "Most of the large brands today have a Rivigo fleet. When we launched a program where we had to attach fleets to a network, we didn't have to train many people on our technology because most fleet supervisors were ex-Rivigo," Garg says.

LEVERAGING THE POWER OF SCALE TO
REIMAGINE SUPPLY CHAINS

When COVID-19 hit India, Garg's phone rang incessantly as worried CEOs, chairpersons, and promoters of companies called him to understand the impact the pandemic would have on their supply chains. In response, Rivigo began running "Reimagine Supply Chain" conclaves for its customers, which even the government of India sent representatives to for two sessions.

"Overall, the supply chain has gotten more important with time," Garg says. "In the '80s and '90s manufacturing was the biggest bottleneck in India, and most of the board members in an organization came from that sector. In the 2000s, it was sales. The pandemic has ensured the next couple of decades will see supply chain managers at the forefront."

Garg acknowledges the growing importance of digitalization in the industry, and how it is improving connectivity between end-to-end supply chain stakeholders. "Documents are now processed electronically. We see electric trucks on the roads today. People are becoming more conscious and committed to change. Companies are envisioning a better, safer, and healthier world. Slowly but steadily, more and more people are hopping on to the digital investment bandwagon."

Sitting at ground zero of that change in India, Garg contends that the country's trucking industry faces some existential questions. "We have not added capacity for the last few years, but considering our demands are going through the roof, we're forced to do that now. That said, new trucks are very expensive today. Many companies don't realize it now, but India will shift from a buyer market to a supply market soon, and this phase will last for the next decade."

That shift has already begun. While the Indian government lowered new equipment prices by reducing taxes, shippers were surprised that the freight prices continued to hold up. To alleviate that pressure, Rivigo built the National Freight Index (NFI), an open-source data portal that provides daily spot freight rates across lanes in the country with a high level of accuracy, helping detect turning points and enabling various stakeholders in the logistics industry to keep track of where the market is heading.

"We noticed that buyers [primarily] faced two kinds of problems in the freight market — pricing transparency and capacity quality," notes Garg. "Getting the right supply quality at the right price is the top priority. A lot of haggling and bargaining goes into achieving this. Keeping this in mind, we built the NFI portal to establish trust and transparency in the industry. After we launched it, every person I talked to in the market — be it brokers, freight buyers, or suppliers — referred to Rivigo's data portal for their business," asserts Garg.

THE MARKERS OF THE QUINTESSENTIAL SUPPLY CHAIN LEADER

Helpfully, as the need for good supply chain leadership grows Garg attests that these roles, and the people who fill them, have evolved over time. Whereas a supply chain leader was traditionally a head of logistics, dealing primarily with transportation cost and SLA management, they have now become a head of supply chain — a role that has a much broader scope and, ergo, increased control over the supply chain.

"Previously, the supply chain was all about handling costs and reducing operational expenses. But now, it encompasses end-to-end fulfillment. I've seen this transition in India, thanks to e-commerce. Today, people with amazing leadership skills occupy this position," Garg says. "Even as the world moves from manufacturing to sales to the supply chain, our people are responsible for delivering a good customer experience, ensuring fulfillment, and optimizing cost, among other functions.

"Since supply chain leadership has become a critical role, its arche-type needs to change. A person in this position needs to have skill sets matching the level of the CEO's. They need to manage an organization's inventory and delivery. They need to handle everyday disruptions. In the next few years, it's their responsibility to figure out the supply chain footprint, both operationally and tactically."

Garg believes anyone with an analytical mindset and the will to learn on the job every day would perform well in supply chain management. "Today's supply chain is not just functional, but is also integrated into every other process in the organization. You need to have good operational, data, and technology skills to integrate everything with the supply chain. You can't just be a good sales guy or a good finance guy in this industry."

At Rivigo, Garg focuses on these intrinsically when hiring. "Our hiring strategy is driven by how a candidate fits our leadership principles, and not just skills and capabilities. We also cross-hire manufacturing people from Indian FMCG companies, as talent can be found anywhere."

"I'd say exposure is the prime need today. Exposure guarantees you a lot of learning. It builds your learning ability, muscle, and capability. It also gives you choices on what you want to pursue as a specialization in your career; something you can focus on. A career in the supply chain gives you just that: a 360-degree view of a business, and for someone who enjoys being at that vantage point there's no better choice than the supply chain as a place of work."

Scan the QR code below or visit www.sourcetosold.com to access exclusive bonus content you can use with your teams to further explore the concepts and insights covered in this book.

CHAPTER 8:

DIRK HOLBACH

"A good supply chain leader needs to exercise mental stability, be able to pivot on the spot, nurture creativity, and foster a forward-looking attitude."

Dirk Holbach is corporate senior vice president and chief supply chain officer of the consumer brands division (beauty, laundry, home care) at Düsseldorf-based Henkel. He began his career at the company in 1996 as junior manager of corporate purchasing, moved up to become head of laundry and home care purchasing in 2004, and rose through the ranks to hold a series of high-level supply chain positions prior to his current role, which comes with a remit that covers six regional hubs, forty-four factories and 150 warehouses.

Before entering supply chain, Dirk Holbach had planned for a career in the automotive industry, in line with his academic credentials in mechanical engineering: "I largely shaped my learning around industry internships, which led me to lean more on the technical side," he recalls. But that plan went south after he graduated in the mid-'90s, as the automotive industry in Germany was in bad shape and hiring was at an all-time low. Compelled to look for opportunities elsewhere, Holbach started a job in the procurement division at Henkel.

"I worked in corporate purchasing, a completely new role back then, with a small team that had recently started to globalize," he says.

"From setting up the first global price controlling tool for the group to organizing the team, it was my first stint at leading supply chain operations at a global level."

About a decade into his career, Holbach arrived at a crossroads, with options to either move toward a B2B leadership role or head into supply chain operations. "I picked the latter, and it became the guiding light to my career," he says. "I kept filling new positions that allowed me to transform and shape my organization and my area of responsibility. I stepped into laundry and home care in 2008 and took on more responsibility to transform its supply chain. Fast forward to today, and I've been running the global supply chain operations for Henkel's laundry and home care business unit since 2014 and most recently took over responsibility for the newly formed Henkel Consumer Brands business unit."

For Holbach, the supply chain is clearly the place to be. "I enjoy being part of it, as it's a people business. Of course, we talk about processes day in and day out, but at the end of the day, it's more about the people — your stakeholders, partners, and colleagues. And it's a comprehensive business. If you want it to work in synchronization along the value chain, you need to associate all the elements together, be it product design, planning, sourcing, delivering, and even managing returns."

THE MENTAL PROWESS THAT DEFINES A SUPPLY CHAIN LEADER

"I think broad knowledge and experience is the number-one foundational quality of a good supply chain leader," contends Holbach. "At Henkel, we usually don't hire people on the go. We educate our future supply chain leaders in different roles, functions, and competencies along the value chain. If someone comes from a manufacturing or a technical background, we teach them how the logistics part of the organization works."

While Holbach concedes that grooming people for specific roles within the supply chain takes time, he argues that it pays dividends long after. "People we've trained in the last 15 years are now capable of overseeing a broad range of activities within the industry, and are well-equipped with the skills and experience needed to make decisions."

> "The leader needs to convert issues and catastrophes into opportunities, create a mid- to long-term vision of where the supply chain needs to be, develop a course for reaching there, and pull the organization along with them."

Beyond skills and experience, having the right personality — whether in terms of mentality or approach — is equally important. Holbach contends that the complexity of the supply chain demands people with a high level of personal resilience. "A good supply chain leader needs to exercise mental stability, be able to pivot on the spot, nurture creativity, and foster a forward-looking attitude. It's about having the right temperament to not resign when problems arise, and, equally, not relying exclusively on past experience — things nowadays develop too fast into new territories, which requires different approaches.

"The leader needs to convert issues and catastrophes into opportunities, create a mid- to long-term vision of where the supply chain needs to be, develop a course for reaching there, and pull the organization along with them. Alongside this, they should also react to smaller blips and catastrophic events, like the Suez Canal crisis or the pandemic crisis. The lesson here is to be agile, as you can't stay prepared for everything that comes your way."

Holbach draws parallels between a supply chain leader and the captain of a ship: while there are several courses for a vessel to reach its destination, the onus is on the captain to study the maps and navigate the best course. "There could be wild weather, and the captain will have to fine-tune his tactics to ensure there's no damage. That's similar to being the head of the supply chain — you have to continuously adjust your strategies to stay on course in the best possible way."

But beyond the integrity of the leader and the team, the environment they work in also plays a part in ensuring a resilient supply chain. Having the right infrastructure, systems, and processes in place helps a leader control the intricacies of running the supply chain, enabling them to make appropriate decisions even on short notice.

"Supply chains run on huge production lines that can be stretched to a point where nothing happens. But often, overdoing the smallest of elements in a certain area collapses the entire system, which takes a long time to recover," Holbach says. "As a supply chain leader, you need to understand your people and systems and how they work together. This enables you to forecast the impact of your decisions, and equips you with the ability to evaluate its consequences."

Having worked all over the world, Holbach grasps the importance of this latter principle more than most. "Before I step into a different country, I spend time understanding its context and sensitivities. I've learned this while working in Asia, which is a melting pot of different countries, cultures, and social backgrounds.

"While working there, I made sure I engaged with my colleagues and talked about the dos and don'ts of the place. You must learn the different ways of engaging with people and use them to your advantage. Of course, everyone makes mistakes once in a while, but you need to learn from your mistakes and adjust your behavior accordingly while staying true to yourself."

Holbach explains that his leadership philosophy is predicated on placing the right people in the right roles and empowering teams, with the goal of ensuring that everyone is engaged in such a manner that it's easier to achieve the agreed-upon target. "People call this 'servant leadership,' which enables everyone in the team to do their best for the company, the business, and themselves. I'm a huge proponent of this method, as it keeps everyone happy where they are."

RECRUITING SUPPLY CHAIN TALENT THAT CAN MAKE A DIFFERENCE

One of the long-standing issues within the supply chain is the lack of enough qualified talent entering the industry. Holbach contends that one of the primary reasons for this is an educational system that does not guarantee a direct inflow of ready-made supply chain talent.

"The supply chain is so broad and complex that it comparatively needs more time and exposure for young professionals to adapt to their roles than for other job profiles in the industry," he says. "This is an extra angle we stress when engaging with young university talents. We also actively seek people from different age groups, as talent cohorts from every generation bring something new to the table — be it with their interests, or their perspective on how they'd contribute to the business."

As an example, Holbach cites sustainability, a subject which some companies are vocal and enthusiastic about while others do not evince a similar zeal. Holbach argues that those in the latter group miss out on attracting the younger talent pool, because this generation holds sustainability as a profoundly personal value. By offering the correct propositions on this issue, companies can engage this up-and-coming cohort at a deeper level.

"We have built a system of recruiting new talent that has worked for us over the last few years," Holbach relates. "We have a list of universities we regularly visit and engage with the students through seminars. We give them an open floor to talk to us. We create an ecosystem where we converse with young professionals and explain to them the benefits of working in the supply chain. This usually gets them interested in joining us, and helps us attract valuable young resources."

For better or for worse, supply chains have received a lot of coverage in the mainstream media in recent years due to the unique challenges that businesses have encountered in the pandemic era. Holbach contends that while some people could simply conclude from this that supply chains are a mess and aren't working as they should, others could see it as an opportunity to go out there and do something about it.

"Such exposure was previously unheard of, but is now working in our favor," Holbach claims. "As professionals in the supply chain industry, we need to leverage it to attract more people. People are finally curious, and want to see how they can contribute to such a situation."

Regarding talent recruitment, Holbach's advice is to look at the wider context of a candidate's experiences, rather than nitpick about the precise talent fit. "Context is important, as anyone interested and willing to learn can do well in the supply chain. You need to recruit characteristically smart people with the right attitude, and place them in the right roles. This can't be said of a technical role, as the harder the technicalities associated with a role get, the more difficult it is to broaden the scope of the talent pool."

BOLSTERING SUPPLY CHAINS TO IMPROVE RESILIENCE TO DISRUPTION

The COVID-19 pandemic was a game changer for many companies, teaching them that the innately complex supply chains that they so often took for granted are, in reality, forever balanced on a knife's edge. "Post-COVID, the industry realized that any supply and value chain is only as strong as its weakest link," Holbach says. "With the number of links in a complicated supply network, even one link breaking down creates a massive problem. This puts the role of a global supply chain leader in the spotlight. Not many roles are as intellectually challenging, and its complexity increases every passing day."

The catastrophic pressure on supply chains raised tensions, as the top management demanded answers to questions hitherto never discussed. Holbach argues that this was a much-needed learning process. "We deployed a corrective action plan when the crisis hit, and we were good to go. But challenges continue to persist, and the techniques to deal with them have also changed over time.

"Today, everyone realizes how vital supply chains are to business success. You can produce the best products, deploy the greatest marketing concepts, have the best R&D team in place, but if you aren't running an effective supply chain and practicing continuous replenishment to satisfy market demand, all of this is in vain. Supply chains are finally being seen as the engine to enable sustainable growth, and supply chain professionals are using this to define their roles more comprehensively."

Holbach fully believes these changes are not temporary, and are likely to persist in the aftermath of the pandemic and geopolitical disruptions. Add sustainability to this equation, and companies are on the verge of massive transformations unlike anything they have experienced before. To fully realize these benefits, however, companies looking to build forward-looking supply chains will have to invest in the right people, processes, and technology.

THE SYSTEMATIC APPROACH TO STAYING RELEVANT

Holbach opines that a supply chain leader's priority should be to stay curious, as learning new things and shaping different outcomes will help them grow in their career. "I've always been driven by the intent and the desire to optimize processes, as I'm continuously looking for ways to do things better, nicer, and cheaper. As a leader looking at the future, I must stay self-motivated and grow according to the latest developments."

This includes fostering connections and networking with like-minded people in the industry. Holbach says that he maintains a continuous dialogue with supply chain leaders in other companies, people in academia, and consultants at management consulting firms in order to keep himself abreast of industry happenings. "Of course it's not always easy, especially in the current circumstances, as I'm always caught up in solving day-to-day crises," he says. "But I manage to stay updated by exercising a decent level of personal discipline. You must force yourself to dedicate some time to the future-shaping elements of your work."

For outsiders to the field it can be a real challenge to understand and appreciate the dense network of flows and interfaces that every supply chain is built on, whereas people within the supply chain intrinsically understand that the answer to a customer's question of "Why has my product not arrived?" is often not a simple one. "Supply chains are incredibly complex," attests Holbach. "Missing a specific product component can chalk up delays and create bottlenecks that can't be dislodged for months. Issues can flare up across various segments, from supplies to transport to the labor market. These constraints are built on top of each other, and are so interconnected that there is no one thing you can do to solve them.

"The answer is always a combination of measures. I've observed that this interdependency is something that people who are outsiders to the supply chain industry find hard to grasp and appreciate. They believe it's about putting more people or money into the system to have it up and running again, but we know that isn't how supply chains work."

Nonetheless, the situation is slowly changing. Holbach is positive that businesses are now treading carefully, diligently studying their supply chains before going in and altering their delicate balance. "Businesses are not exclusively looking to cut costs on their supply chains, which is a promising start. They are against one-sided saving on resources, capacity, and capabilities in their supply chains. They are starting to see that the larger the business, the more they've got to invest into keeping the supply chain working seamlessly.

"I think supply chains have entered a renaissance period, and things will likely continue to look up in the future."

Scan the QR code below or visit www.sourcetosold.com to access exclusive bonus content you can use with your teams to further explore the concepts and insights covered in this book.

CHAPTER 9:

IVANKA JANSSEN

"Be curious, and dare to put yourself in situations that will challenge you at work."

Ivanka Janssen has been the EVP and chief supply chain officer at Philips, a leading health technology company, since January 2021. She joined the organization in 2019 as SVP of global integrated supply chain, operating out of Hong Kong. Prior to Philips she worked in the Swiss office of PepsiCo as VP of supply chain for Europe, Eastern Europe and Sub-Saharan Africa, and she has also held senior supply chain positions with market-leading firms Diageo and Altria. Her educational background is in Economics and Law, MBA and she pursued a master in logistics.

As with so many others in the field, Ivanka Janssen did not forge her way through supply chain as the result of a consciously thought-out career plan. "My educational background is in economics and law. I pursued a master's in logistics, but it was about identifying locations to build airports and seaports. Luckily, when it was time to find a job, I came across a traineeship in the port of Rotterdam, which sounded exciting. And that's where my career in supply chain took off."

"I find supply chain to be very hands-on and an adventurous function where there's never a dull moment. It requires you to be resilient and cope with a lot of pressure, and that's where everything comes together. You need to keep a cool head and oversee end-to-end operations without panicking when certain segments are not working as intended."

Janssen got a crash course in that scenario immediately upon taking over the role of chief supply chain officer at Philips in the first month of the pandemic, which brought about crises that spanned supply chain nodes. Even as the company was forced to scale down part of its business, as demand initially dropped due to the closure of brick-and-mortar shops, other business segments increased, pushing Janssen and her team to ramp up operations to fulfill demand. However, those scaling-up measures were fraught with chaos, as the rash of pandemic-shuttered businesses limited the supply of critical components essential to manufacturing.

Despite these challenges, Janssen and her team were able to persevere thanks to their skill at building connections. "Once we sourced the components, we had to ship them. And with transportation networks being fragile, we had to bring them all together while staying composed. The whole situation around the pandemic led us to forge amazing partnerships with suppliers, be it in setting up an air bridge or sourcing components," she says. "These partnerships mean a lot, as streamlining sourcing operations quickly during the pandemic can't be done without help."

Within Philips, the pandemic necessitated that the company shore up resources and step away from some traditional ways of working. Janssen split logistics operations across tribes and squads made up of people from different sectors across the organization, with each small team responsible for a certain stream of activities. "Let's say one tribe was responsible for ventilators — that tribe had several squad teams, each squad team focusing on specific parts or components such as filters or tubes," she explains.

Janssen stresses that these teams functioned with no established organizational hierarchy, as they were not assigned supervisors — rather, they had tribe or squad leaders who contributed collectively, and then consolidated or streamlined updates that would then be sent to top management. This "flat" hierarchy allowed the organization to stay agile while ensuring employees remained motivated to continue working through such uncertain times.

"The teams truly proved to us as a company that integrated teams and flat organizations can empower people and provide them the freedom to shape their tribe or squad in the way they see fit," Janssen says. "This unleashed a lot of power, energy, and creativity. As with every company we had several people that suffered from COVID, but this move helped us power through even in their absence."

SUPPLY CHAIN AS A PRIMARY TOUCHPOINT

"If you think of the supply chain, we are the first ones to make contact with the customer after the sales process is over," Janssen says. "We take the order, fine-tune it with the customer, and ensure we deliver the order. In a nutshell, it's all about customer satisfaction and delivering upon our promises."

As they regulate the central artery that connects a multitude of operations, supply chain leaders have an unparalleled overview of the entire organization, according to Janssen. "In a way, we can feel the pulse of the organization. I can tell you, at any point in time, how our order book is developing, where we are on fulfilling our delivery promises to our customer, or where we are heading in the next eighteen to twenty-four months. It's about the end-to-end visibility supply chain has into the organization's performance at any given moment."

"Where we need to do better is in explaining how the supply chain works to colleagues in the organization. With better understanding, we will have increased collaboration across the value chain, helping maximize output."

Janssen contends that creating transparency across the organization allows management to respond quickly to disruption, be it with component shortages or logistics bottlenecks. "Supply chain is still often seen as a cost factor only, doing its job behind the scenes. I believe COVID has brought the importance of supply chain more into the limelight, where it is not only about costs, but [about using] the end-to-end overview and the insights into trends coming well in advance. These insights can be collectively leveraged by the organization, and strategies built around it."

"Where we need to do better is in explaining how the supply chain works to colleagues in the organization. With better understanding, we will have increased collaboration across the value chain, helping maximize output. For example, you see this reflected in our sales and operations planning process, which we are bringing to a next level. Knowing the short- and mid-term forecast, the lead times on materials and logistical challenges, means that together we can determine how different scenarios play out and decide [what to do]."

TECHNOLOGY AT THE FOREFRONT

For Janssen, the continuation of the digitalization trend is important. "For example, we are seeing good results in improving our fore-casting accuracy with the use of artificial intelligence and machine learning. [But] after our first pilot, an important learning was to spend more time on engaging people in the journey and what it would mean for their work."

Janssen explains that while some people are excited using new technologies, others find it harder to let go of traditional processes and the way of working they are familiar with. "While most people do eagerly adopt digitalization, there are always a few that are more hesitant [about] change. Demystifying technology and educating people about what happens in the supply chain is vital."

Janssen stresses the importance of being constantly exposed to innovation in the industry. She cites how she looks to stay current by conversing with thought leaders and fellow executives from comparably large organizations, but also notes that, "I also connect with start-ups, as they can be extremely innovative in finding solutions for long-standing problems.

"As an organization, we try to stimulate people to come up with innovative ideas on how we can make the business better," she continues. "We are developing a company-wide program that is supply chain-specific, teaching employees the skills we need and giving them opportunities to change their career path if they wish."

Even as she helps to ensure that the company continues to empower workers with upskilling opportunities, Janssen points out that the automation of repetitive manual work will continue to progress. "There are still many opportunities to automate manual work in organizations today," she says. "It helps to speed up operations, brings agility and reduces the risk of manual errors creeping in. Automation can help here, like with the use of robotic process automation [RPA]."

BEING CURIOUS AND WALKING THE TALK

"I read an awful lot on what's out there to stay updated in the industry and encourage my peers and teams at the company to do so. Reading and learning are helpful," Janssen says. "And learning need not be formalized — you can do a lot to educate and develop yourself."

Within Philips, Janssen has helped introduce coding courses across the entire organization, and has enrolled herself in the course as well. After opening with a batch of roughly 450 people, the course doubled its enrolment with its second batch, which promises much for its continued success. "While I helped create context for flagging off such courses, it is a group of young, talented people who set up the entire program and continue to make it successful," Janssen says. "Instead of having a generic register-and-train system, this helped foster a community where even people from outside the supply chain segment showed interest in being a part of it."

On the hiring front, Janssen highlights the need to recruit the right talent and to ensure diversity within the organization: "I'm a fierce advocate for diversity, be it with gender, ethnicity, social background, age, or experience." Attesting to that commitment, she and her peers created a network for women leaders in supply chain. "We were time and again pushed to demonstrate our leadership capabilities more than our male counterparts, and it usually was an unconscious process," she says. "Although there has been much progress, I still believe it benefits from constructive attention."

"At Philips we are addressing this not just in the supply chain, but also across the board. We have a group of senior female leaders that are developing programs to create awareness on unconscious biases that lead people to behave differently — be it with a man, a woman, or someone of a minority group. We need to embrace inclusion and diversity, and walk the talk. Personally, I find it liberating to have a balanced team around me who think differently. Collective thinking enriches the team — you become more productive, and it's fun."

When asked what has contributed to her longevity in the business, Janssen attributes it to following her passion and making a living out of it. "Life will be much easier if you follow your heart and work on your passion," she says. "Be curious, and dare to put yourself in situations that will challenge you at work. Enhance your resilience by getting a complete, enterprise-wide view of operations. If you enjoy being in the supply chain and working outside your comfort zone, I trust you will find a way to climb up the ladder, or maybe even grow into areas you would have never expected to work in."

Scan the QR code below or visit www.sourcetosold.com to access exclusive bonus content you can use with your teams to further explore the concepts and insights covered in this book.

CHAPTER 10:

ANDREAS KRINNINGER

"Collaboration is of higher value than ongoing firefighting."

Andreas Krinninger has spent over a decade at KION Group AG in Frankfurt, Germany, having first joined the multinational manufacturing and services firm in 2011 as chief restructuring officer. He subsequently took on the roles of CFO and CEO of KION subsidiary Linde Material Handling, and now sits on KION's executive board as well as serving as president of the industrial trucks and services division for Europe, the Middle East and Africa (EMEA). Prior to joining KION, he supported KKR's private equity portfolio as Director at its operational division Capstone in London, worked as chief supply chain officer for Grohe AG in Düsseldorf, led global operational excellence at LSG SkyChefs as senior vice president in Dallas, and spent six years as a project manager for McKinsey & Company.

Even compared to the many other executives in the industry who have not pursued a straight-line path into supply chain, Andreas Krinninger is notable for having transitioned across roles and industries that are starkly different from each other. "But just having a fully laden CV doesn't magically make every step along the way a success story" he laughs.

While he was still in elementary school, Krinninger spent many nights gazing at the moon with his uncle, who had been the project leader for NASA's lunar rover. "At this point, I got this burning desire from him to do something that has lasting value — to leave behind more than what I've received in my life."

Immediately after finishing his master's degree at MIT and RWTH Aachen, he went to work for McKinsey & Company and sought out those projects that aimed to provide meaningful contributions to companies' bottom and top lines. "I quickly got exposed to a very diverse environment. In the six years I was there I [saw] every stage of a project come to life, from concept to implementation. It was personally important to me, as I truly wanted to see what works and what doesn't," he comments.

With this vantage point over end-to-end operations, Krinninger came to understand how business strategy drives operations strategy, which eventually becomes an enabler to competitive differentiation. "There is more than one way to create value in a supply chain, and, at the end, achieve the best result for the customer. While supply chain operations need to be robust, precise, and reliable [in order] for companies to succeed, solving the complexities that arise within the system is also critical. That is what truly makes a difference in the market."

OPTIMIZING SUPPLY CHAINS BY CREATING COLLECTIVE VALUE

In Krinninger's opinion, "uniting behind one opportunity and one target within supply chains is one of our biggest challenges. It requires people to band together and understand the contribution of every individual in the team, and how this can translate into collective value for the organization. It is very important to understand [that] collaboration is of higher value than ongoing firefighting."

To illustrate the importance of finding systemic solutions rather than quick fixes, Krinninger recalls one time when he had to solve a problem in which a company running a made-to-order business found itself running out of stock, which led them to quickly ramp up inventory. "While you can do this to an extent, it's obviously costly in terms of the inventory you build up, as there's always a risk that you produced the wrong inventory or in excess," says Krinninger. "In our case, though, it did give us the time required to work on the strategic level of significantly shortening the lead time — from four weeks, to a week, to a few days. On the other end of the spectrum, you [should] also look to get more accurate information from the sales side to complement efficiency increase upstream."

THE CHALLENGE OF CREATING A LASTING IMPACT

As a McKinsey consultant who was external to his clients' organizations, Krinninger could only exert so much influence over the employees. It was this recurring obstacle that ultimately compelled him to make a concerted move into the field himself. "I saw a myriad of implementation challenges, which led me to switch from consultancy to the industry, as I felt I had a different level of influence in an organization. I could develop people and companies, and that felt right."

Since making his move, Krinninger has worked in many diverse environments in supply chain and operations, from heading an airline catering business with LSG SkyChefs, to acting as CSCO for home-fitting solutions provider Grohe, to serving as CEO at Linde Material Handling . And it was precisely through this diversity of experience that he was able to create the long-lasting impact he'd always strived for.

> "Luck is a combination of acquiring
> capabilities and creating opportunities."

"A lot of people ask me how I successfully transitioned to different industries and companies in my career. I'd say it's about creating opportunities for yourself by delivering in positions you're in

— trying to impact, exchange ideas, and grow. Some say that these opportunities are luck. But I think luck is a combination of acquiring capabilities and creating opportunities. It's easy to call this luck, but there's more to it than meets the eye.

"I believe that taking different perspectives helps you learn so much from one segment to the other because there are always certain similarities. I think this aspect helps you get more precise in your analysis of what needs to be done, how it can be done, and the ways to equip people to get that done."

Krinninger's long journey within supply chain has afforded him the time and experience to crystallize metrics that can create real change in a company. "What does it take, really? I'd say it's a combination of analytical thinking and an uncanny skill to solve problems. Being a 'people leader' is essential, and so is the ability to coax people into [being proud of] being part of a great organization."

CUSTOMER SATISFACTION IS WHAT DRIVES SUPPLY CHAINS

Fundamentally, supply chains exist for a single purpose: ensuring that end users get their needs delivered to them. It's for this reason that sales and supply chain need to work hand in hand. While sales is the first point of contact with a customer, a transaction can only be deemed successful when supply chains follow up and deliver the sales proposition. The cardinal function of supply chains in this process is to secure deliverables of the appropriate quality and deliver them on time.

As Krinninger explains, designing a supply chain that can success-fully back up claims from the sales department is not easy, because every industry has its own particularities. "[First], you need to define what the supply chain needs to be good at," he says. "What's the metric you're designing it to excel [at]? Is it about being fast or more reliable? Is it about managing a high level of complexity? Is it about manufacturing products that are beyond standard configurations?

"Supply chains can't be good at every aspect. There are always trade-offs in the supply chain. Understanding where you can best satisfy your customer and how you can best differentiate against the competition is critical."

Krinninger recalls an instance during his McKinsey days when he was working as a consultant for a trailer manufacturing company. When he was introduced to the company's business, the standard delivery lead times for their trailers were in the range of ten to twelve weeks. However, this could balloon to nearly six months depending on the design complexity and customization options.

"While working for them, we figured that they could make their way into markets they hadn't thought about before. Speed to customer was of the essence. This was a spot business, so when you have repetitive business alongside the spot, you are in a better position to ramp up capacity quickly. Eventually, we were able to reduce lead times from several months to a week, and then to eighteen hours."

The new market that Krinninger introduced the client to was truck trailer rentals — the company could beat rental companies to the punch by producing truck trailers faster than any rental company could provide them to the customer. Aside from lowering costs, Krinninger also helped automate the majority of the company's administrative processes. The result was a lean, efficiently functioning business with extremely short lead times, in which processing time and product cost were both significantly reduced.

BUILDING SEAMLESS SUPPLY CHAINS TO MAXIMIZE EFFICIENCY

"People in supply chains could learn a lot from an orchestra," observes Krinninger. "A supply chain built like an orchestra would mean everyone knows what to do, how to do it, and at what point in time they have to do it. I remember some benchmark visits to a Toyota plant in Japan, where you can see that there's no variance in the process of how they do things. It's a highly optimized and standardized environment with a sense of calm built into the system."

At one point in his career, Krinninger was an executive in the airline catering industry, working with different airline carriers to ensure operations ran smoothly and on time. "Airline food was of two kinds," he remembers. "The one at the lower end for the economy class, where you provide food that satisfies the minimum calorie requirements on a tight budget; and then you have the business and first class, where people get better meals."

The need to offer best-in-class food for passengers flying at a premium led Krinninger to work with Michelin-star chefs. "I had the pleasure of working with Alain Ducasse, the only chef to run three three-Michelin-star restaurants across two continents. Having three such restaurants would mean you must have an incredible consistency in your operations and deliver the same quality across every single meal.

"Once, we were sitting in one of his restaurants in Paris, a space with the kitchen viewable to the diners behind a glass wall. And then out came the waiters, as you'd see in a ballet. There was no yelling, no jostling, and no running into each other — they were completely in sync. Operations meets cuisine."

This, Krinninger contends, is the key to smooth operations. It is not about applying brute force, but rather a matter of meticulously working to remove variances from the process, followed by deft coordination of the component parts. Achieving this level of synchronicity is especially valuable when facing chaotic, disruptive events like the COVID-19 pandemic.

As an executive on the board of KION Group, the largest material-handling equipment provider in the world, Krinninger had a ringside view for what played out during the 2020 lockdown. "What fascinates me about supply chains is that we keep the world moving, whatever happens. We helped customers ramp up operations, which saw orders going through the roof via e-commerce channels. We solved operational bottlenecks and provided additional capacity.

"I think that's a great purpose to have, being a part of the supply chain and serving societies. We are the connecting tissue between a business and its customers, which gives us great insight into what the future holds for the company. I feel there's nothing more exciting than building a supply chain that runs incredibly stable and reliable operations — just like a three-Michelin-star restaurant would."

Scan the QR code below or visit www.sourcetosold.com to access exclusive bonus content you can use with your teams to further explore the concepts and insights covered in this book.

CHAPTER 11:

JAY LEE

"As a leader, you don't just make continuous improvement: you disrupt the system."

Jay Lee is Ohio Eminent Scholar and Founding Director of the Industrial AI Center as well as the Intelligence Maintenance Systems (IMS) Center — formerly a multi-campus National Science Foundation (NSF) Industry/University Cooperative Research Center (I/UCRC) led by the University of Cincinnati. He serves as a senior adviser to McKinsey & Company, is a member of the Global Future Council on Production of the World Economic Council, and also served as vice chairman and a member of the board of Foxconn Technology Group during from 2019 to 2021.

As the world's largest provider of electronics manufacturing services, with almost a million employees on payroll and operations that involve materials procurement of over $100 billion annually, Foxconn has built a reputation for running extremely precise supply chain operations. But accordingly, the scale and intricacy of that supply chain means that it is also one of the first companies to feel the heat when disruption rears its head, which Jay Lee has seen plenty of over the years.

"Global supply chain issues are in the spotlight [now], as they are not one-time issues. Think of it as a spring — they compress and depress, but they don't disappear," he says. "For instance, the COVID-19 pandemic fueled a semiconductor-chip crisis right at the time when there was a boost in consumerism, which [is something] we had to tackle at Foxconn."

Lee attributes his facility in improving supply chains to the experiences he has gained while shuttling between the corporate world and academia. "In engineering terms, I like to put my career through a metal treatment procedure: I've alternated between melting at high temperatures in an industrial environment, [and then] quenching it in the cool waters of academia. This strengthened my career, molding it into what I can do today."

Lee describes the practical application of his doubled perspective as a three-step process. "[First], I look at the industries around me to find technological blind spots. I then look at the processes that should be improved but aren't. [Finally], I use my academic knowledge to fill this gap. Being in academia has helped me see these industrial gaps and equipped me to fill them. It helps me give direction to my career."

"Foxconn was an important milestone, because it gave me a platform to expose myself to the corporate world. Not only did I get to use my academic knowledge to improve operations, but it also gave me a good idea to visualize what the next ten to twenty years in technology will look like."

BUILDING RESILIENCE IN SUPPLY CHAIN BY FILLING OPERATIONAL GAPS

To consistently enhance operational resilience, it is critical to seek out the inefficiencies within the system, Lee declares. Once these are identified, he advocates that companies should take a rational approach to address them, choosing solutions based on the fundamental nature of the problem. "[For example], manufacturing companies that rely on human-centric operations will have to deal with labor gaps in the system by recruiting assembly workers, and not think of substituting worker shortage with automation. While automation is great, it isn't a be-all-end-all solution — certainly not at the cost of breaking down an entire process chain."

Lee stresses the need to have a top-to-bottom approach when addressing systemic inefficiencies, establishing a hierarchy of needs to determine the urgency with which each should be addressed. "Once you identify a major gap, you must put them in one of [the] quadrants based on the frequency of occurrence and criticality. If it's a high-frequency, high-criticality issue, you need to implement prompt solutions. If it's high-frequency, low-criticality, you can take a while — but not too long. If it's low in frequency but highly critical, you need to handle it through continuous monitoring. Low-frequency, less critical problems are best left alone."

Such a systematic approach to addressing supply chain problems can prevent particular issues from snowballing into something more significant over time. "During the pandemic, we realized that employees didn't want to involve themselves in operations that require touching surfaces," recalls Lee. "This was a high-frequency, high-criticality issue, and so we immediately tried solving it by bringing in automation to replace touch with gestures like hand-waving. Your solutions should be such that they minimize the problem and make the production process safer."

Lee equates end-to-end supply chains to the journey food takes from farm to fork. "You source vegetables from the farmer much like you source raw materials in the supply chain. The produce is stored and sold in the food market, which in our case is the warehouse; our service factories are our kitchens. And just like a shortage of produce in the kitchen can create a meal imbalance, supply chain shortage can create a market imbalance. If you don't have enough ingredients, you can't cook good food, much like a shortage of raw materials can stop us from creating finished products. Restaurants are forced to raise their prices to match rising food expenses; similarly, businesses have to jack up prices to meet rising supply chain costs."

As gaps in the system can disrupt this chain, it is therefore in a company's best interests to constantly ensure that operations run smoothly both in-house and further downstream. "If your food supply is broken, your restaurant suffers. If the supply chain is broken, your business suffers," Lee says.

THE STRUCTURED APPROACH TO SUPPLY CHAIN LEADERSHIP

Lee asserts that a supply chain leader finds their purpose through discovering problems in operations, and then working toward solving them. "It could be as simple as resolving a customer complaint or bringing visibility into freight movement. The idea is to put things in perspective and solve problems in a way that aligns with your purpose," he says.

"I call it the Three-P approach. The first P is your problems, some of which you can minimize and others which are out of your control. The second P is your purpose, which tells you where you're going. The third P is the process that helps you establish your standard internal SOPs.

"The three Ps flow in that order. Your purpose drives the processes you use to solve your problems, not the other way around. This approach helps me transition across different roles with conviction."

Lee expresses surprise at how, in his opinion, many leaders place greater value in position than in purpose. "When I see their business cards, they define their roles based on their designations," he says. "For example, a 'project manager' title doesn't tell me anything about what they do. They should change it to 'purpose management,' and add a purpose percentage to it. If their purpose is a 10 percent process improvement, they should call themselves PM 10. That's a much better way to talk about what they do."

"Your purpose drives the processes you use to solve
your problems — not the other way around."

Understanding the purpose of the supply chain is the key to aligning it end to end. "Just like water flows from one point to another, quality flows seamlessly from one quality station to another," Lee explains. "If any of these stations' quality is compromised, it pollutes the entire inventory flow. This is something I've advocated strongly at Foxconn. I look to incentivize their manufacturing management processes, and the same applies to the supply chain."

Along with purpose, supply chain management is also founded upon managing timelines precisely. "Timelines are important, especially in a huge business like Foxconn," Lee says. "When a customer launches its product, we have only a few months to ramp up our production capabilities to enable sales for Christmas. We have to plan everything during this time, from supplier variability to labor management. Depending on the number of pieces and the configurations we're targeting, we make sure the right machines are available in our factories in time to make new products."

Strategic forecasting plays a vital role in keeping operations running strictly on schedule. By way of example, Lee points to the specific questions that need to be answered in advance when hiring a large number of employees to launch new product lines. "What is the exact number we hire? Where do we get them from? Labor is not available easily in most countries. Do you go to a village, and if yes, how do you find people to work there? What happens to these people once you're done with the product launch? If you want to manage your supply chain end to end and effectively, you need to respect the timelines, set the stage right, and ensure there are no surprises.

"These aren't easy questions to answer, but as a supply chain leader, you'll be pressured to make quick decisions and give convincing responses to the board on your choices."

THE NEED TO LOOK AT (AND STRIVE FOR) THE BIG PICTURE

Lee contends that it is vital for supply chain leaders to show subordinates an overarching vision for the company and the impact you want to have on it. "You want them to believe in your vision [so that they can] help turn that into reality," he says. "As a leader, you don't just make continuous improvement: you disrupt the system. It's important to take the top-to-bottom approach with disruption. The support at the top gives you execution power, which you'll have to earn by demonstrating your capabilities. People find it difficult to align with your vision without proof."

As an illustration of this principle, Lee points to his data-supported advocacy for lean manufacturing, which, he contends, can immediately increase profit margins by reducing indirect costs to a business. Through his self-founded company Predictronics — a spin-off from the Intelligence Maintenance System (IMS) Center, a multi-campus NSF Industry/University Cooperative Research Center — Lee uses AI-based predictive analytics solutions to help companies eliminate unplanned downtimes that hamper productivity.

As an example, Lee describes how "Procter & Gamble once struggled to manage the productivity of their diaper line, as they had to frequently clean and restart their machines; we implemented our predictive software, which led to a productivity increase that translated to $450 million in savings per year." Similarly, the implementation of predictive analytics in the compressor system at Toyota Manufacturing in Georgetown, Kentucky has allowed the company to achieve and maintain zero-downtime performance since 2006.

Selecting projects, setting a fixed timeline, and having a concrete roadmap to completion is crucial to driving change, Lee says. Upon joining Foxconn, Lee set a firm goal for himself: to make a major impact on smart manufacturing transformation. In aid of that, he advised Foxconn business units to set up twenty lighthouse factories. "Lighthouses are operational processes within companies with a specific purpose to create new business models," he explains. "They help provide direction to success by basing workflows on the existing use cases, [which drive] real, measurable change in the organization."

Lee also spearheaded the development and construction of the Foxconn Science and Technology Park, a 3,000-acre smart manufacturing center in Mt. Pleasant, Wisconsin, and initiated the stateside manufacturing of servers, which until that point had been predominantly built in China and Mexico. This latter move changed the landscape of the server manufacturing industry, as Foxconn today owns a major share of the production of the server market.

Looking beyond Foxconn, Lee is certainly not lacking in plans for new worlds to conquer. "So far, there are great challenges for yield management in the range of seven-nanometer processes and below, [but] I'm looking to explore the application of our industrial AI to deal with the five- to three-nanometer range," he says. "Another project I'm working on is establishing an electrification program in the university system. Very few people understand how the electric vehicle ecosystem works. These are the two big gaps I want to cover in the next few years.

"If I look at the next ten years, I'd focus on the semiconductor industry," he continues. "I'm looking to build an AI metrology system to help the industry on its frontlines." (Metrology is the science of measurement, which establishes a common understanding of units — something that is fundamental to the engineering of semiconductor chips.)

THE VALUE OF CONTINUOUS LEARNING

For Lee, the mark of a good leader is to stay flexible and resist getting drawn into a comfortable niche. "I stay wary of gravitating into an entitled space in my career for too long. If you stand still and don't continuously learn and develop, you risk staying committed to a certain kind of career," he says.

"We often make the mistake of constraining ourselves based on what we think we can do. "If your academic background revolves around mechanical engineering, you might condition yourself to believe you must deal with mechanical parts all your life. This will [limit] your scope, as you would rarely dare to dream beyond it. Continuous learning gives you choices to explore."

And key to learning, Lee says, is cultivating a mindset that is conducive to multi-disciplinarity. "The right attitude is everything. It lets you learn new things quickly," he explains. "I see people in organizations struggle to understand the concept of a profit margin because they see it [as] something complex. But once they develop the right attitude toward it, they'd realize they don't need a PhD to understand how profit margins come to be. Being an agile and avid learner takes you a long way."

Scan the QR code below or visit www.sourcetosold.com to access exclusive bonus content you can use with your teams to further explore the concepts and insights covered in this book.

CHAPTER 12:

SANDRA MACQUILLAN

"You need both [authenticity and vulnerability] to be a leader people are comfortable working with. However, the levels of authenticity and vulnerability you show around people are critical to ensuring they take you seriously."

Sandra MacQuillan is EVP and chief supply chain officer for global snack industry leader Mondelēz International. She joined Mondelēz in 2019 from Kimberly-Clark, where she served as the company's first-ever supply chain officer and built its supply chain and SC leadership team. Prior to that, she spent more than twenty years at Mars Incorporated in supply chain positions of increasing responsibility around the world, culminating in her appointment as global vice president of supply chain for the firm's pet care business.

When Sandra MacQuillan left Mars Incorporated after two decades with the business, it felt like she was leaving her family. Even though it was a massive confectionary and pet food producer with a stronghold on chocolate manufacturing, Mars was still a privately held family business at the time, and MacQuillan states that during her tenure there she had no intentions of leaving. "Leaving Mars was hard emotionally — like letting your parents down," she says.

"I had spent twenty-one years at Mars at the time I got a phone call from a headhunter. While I refused to check his offer initially, he was persistent, so I finally did budge. This new opportunity was about creating an entire supply chain network for Kimberly–Clark, in a way that cut parallel with what I was doing for the pet care segment within Mars. This excited me."

MacQuillan proceeded to take a meeting with Tom Falk, the then-CEO of Kimberly–Clark. "During the conversation, I remember having this feeling that I could learn a lot from working with him. I could see that Kimberly–Clark was a place where I could continue being stimulated at work. At that point, it wasn't about my career but rather about how well it fits with my values. I felt that if I gave something to the organization, I'd also get something back. This led me to make the jump."

That jump also meant that MacQuillan had to leave Europe for North America — which made the career change a pivotal decision for both MacQuillan and her family, as they would all have to adapt to a new home and way of living. "While we had lived in a lot of places, we still weren't accustomed to the American lifestyle, and it was a bit disconcerting at the start," recalls MacQuillan. "However, I'm always up for a challenge, and the thought that Kimberly–Clark could be an opportunity that was hard to come by made it easier to decide for my family and me."

MANAGING THE WORK CULTURE DIVIDE

As a family-owned business, the working culture at Mars was very different from that of Kimberly–Clark. As she adjusted to her new role, MacQuillan ultimately determined that the best way to acclimatize herself to this new milieu was by putting herself out there and communicating to people how vulnerable she was — an approach that her colleagues reacted to with a mix of shock and surprise.

"I've always been authentic and vulnerable. You need both those qualities to be a leader people are comfortable working with," MacQuillan explains. "However, the *levels* of authenticity and vulnerability you show around people are critical to ensuring they take you seriously. Having spent a lot of my career in a space that's very male-dominated, I had to work that balance carefully."

As MacQuillan notes, that balance is critical for a woman working in supply chain, as showing too much vulnerability will lead people to take advantage of you while maintaining distance could be mistaken for aggression. "This one time, I pushed for people to accept my solution, as I believed what I wanted to do was the right thing," MacQuillan recalls. "But it turned out that the way I went about proving my case was a problem. While I assumed we were tightly bound as an organization, it wasn't that way, and I was considered too aggressive to be pushing for the change I wanted to see in the business."

MacQuillan went back to the drawing board to try and identify the communication gap that she had encountered. "I realized that beneath all of this for me was a feeling of low self-esteem. Even when I was at the leadership level in the organization and had received positive feedback over the years, I still had trouble owning that, and didn't believe in myself to the extent I'd have liked."

This set MacQuillan on a path of self-realization, in the company and with the aid of a life coach. "I think authenticity can be seen in terms of *how* you talk about stuff, and not just what you talk about. I realized that in the past, when I was not successful in a certain situation, I didn't pick up on the signals around me and would continue to fight. That was to prove I *could* do it, not because I'd really thought it through. My coach helped me understand this, and it has impacted how I am [now], in terms of authenticity and vulnerability."

ONGOING AND DIVERSE LEARNING IS CRITICAL

MacQuillan takes learning on the job seriously, and one of the ways she does so is by cultivating connections over social and corporate platforms. "I have a great WhatsApp network with other chief supply chain officers, and also a network of friends who are part of business leadership and advisory boards. Being on external boards myself, I get to learn different things along the way. I've learned a lot about digitalization from being in this environment, which I feel connects nicely to the supply chain."

MacQuillan also believes in surrounding herself with people who have a vision and their own network of connections. "My head of logistics has a fantastic network within the industry. Same with my head of procurement and head of engineering. I'm looking for people who are happy to be out there and to connect with others to learn. They then educate me, which helps me stay on top of stuff. I deliberately ensure I'm bringing in people who have diverse thinking and a great network so that we can keep feeding our in-house knowledge base."

MacQuillan avers that leaders need to ensure they are constantly learning at the workplace and gaining new perspectives. "After setting up the Kimberly–Clark supply chain and ensuring its smooth operations, I felt I had accomplished what I was tasked with at the job. So when I had an opportunity to join Mondelēz and get back to the snack segment in a growth industry, I felt I could move on and experience some new learnings."

At Mondelēz, MacQuillan and her team created a process by which they can identify promising talent and channel them into a development program to help shape them into the supply chain leadership of the future. Yet at the same time, "while rewarding, training, and retaining top talent is critical, so is the environment we are fostering within the organization," MacQuillan insists. "It's not just about what we deliver, but also how we deliver it. At Mondelēz, we are working hard to create a safe space for people to be able to say what they really think — which brings us back to the question of how authentic you can be with your colleagues.

"There's so much happening within supply chains that there are always little cracks here and there within the organization. Though digital connectivity is a thing now, it still isn't ubiquitous, and so people being open to each other will connect us as a team."

"Supply chains work because of its people and its environment; it ceases to exist otherwise."

MacQuillan believes that being a great supply chain leader is about learning to juggle several roles at once. "While we already spoke of authenticity and vulnerability, you also want other qualities, like being pragmatic about everyday operations and having genuine care for your subordinates. If things don't work the way you want them to work, you have to learn to let it go and focus on the positives in order to be a holistic business leader."

"SUPPLY CHAINS ARE THE PLACE TO BE"

For MacQuillan, there's no better place to work than the supply chain. "If you are excited about creating things, working with people, and also having fun while at it, supply chains are the place to be. This segment makes a tangible difference to people's lives, and that's never going to be boring. You go to many places, meet different people, and have a variety of experiences — some good and some bad, but that's what life is all about.

"A well-run supply chain gives its employees security, peace of mind to the investors, and more importantly, helps give back to the environment you're operating in. Supply chains work because of their people and their environment; they cease to exist otherwise."

While MacQuillan is vocal in encouraging women to join the industry, she is of the opinion that mentoring women during their journey through supply chain should not shade over into patronage. "I strongly believe in meritocracy. Being a mentor myself, I push women to be more open and vulnerable about the experiences they've had, which encourages other women to do the same," she states. "I think women in leadership positions today must take the initiative to create connections and talk about how they climbed the ladder. Such anecdotes are compelling."

MacQuillan says that she is often approached by women who have questions about balancing work and family. "They think I have it all, but I tell them that nobody has it all — not even men. If you work a lot, you don't see your family as much as you'd like. These are choices. I've got a supportive husband who decided to stop working before I got pregnant and hasn't gone back to work since. Life is about choices, and you take the ones that seem right for you. If you figure you've taken the wrong route, change it. And that's completely okay."

Scan the QR code below or visit www.sourcetosold.com to access exclusive bonus content you can use with your teams to further explore the concepts and insights covered in this book.

CHAPTER 13:

TAN CHONG MENG

"You will get a lot more mileage in your career if you are propelled by your purpose — don't choose your next step because of a promotion, let the promotion come to you."

Tan Chong Meng is the group CEO of PSA International, a leading global port group and cargo solutions provider in forty-two countries, headquartered in Singapore. He oversees a portfolio comprising sixty-five deep-sea, rail and inland terminals, as well as affiliated businesses in supply chain management, logistics, marine and digital services. Prior to joining PSA in 2011 he spent more than twenty years with the Royal Dutch Shell Group, holding various senior leadership positions that spanned management, sales, marketing, trading, refinery operations, customer service, and mergers and acquisitions involving postings in the US, Europe, China and Singapore.

Having spent over a decade as group CEO of PSA International, a leading global port group and cargo solutions provider, and, prior to that, more than two decades in a global energy and petrochemical conglomerate, Tan Chong Meng can offer well-informed advice on how to climb the ladder. "My first piece of advice would be to not chase promotions," he offers, maintaining that while promotions can be seductive, their long-term promise is debatable. "You will get a lot more mileage in your career if you are propelled by your purpose — don't choose your next step because of a promotion, let the promotion come to you."

Chong Meng experienced one such inflection point in his own career, when he was asked by his company to consider a role that came with an enticing promotion. "That promotion would have pushed me further up the professional track. The role would have made me lean more toward production and away from developing teams, commercial value, and portfolio management. This was an important mid-career choice!" he recalls.

However, after a senior leader counselled him against believing that a promotion was synonymous with furthering his career, Chong Meng, after a lot of thought, declined the offer. "This turned out well. I was approached for a role based in China three months later which was equally if not more attractive, and a role that I was interested in filling. My career took an indelible turn toward my long-term goals after this decision. I learned that not every steppingstone leading you forward is the right one — you have to carefully assess which stone you pick."

"For an aspiring leader, identifying transformative moments within organizations is crucial," Chong Meng points out. "Seeing the potential for transformation and the need for change, building alignment and energizing people to transform the business in these key watershed moments makes a leader." When Chong Meng assumed office as head of PSA International in 2011, he immediately saw that, even though the company ran a global portfolio of ports, it still functioned with a Singapore-centric mindset, which he realized had to change. "More than 50 percent of PSA's volumes came from outside of Singapore. At that time, our ports and terminals business was also being challenged by mega shifts and structural changes in the shipping industry," he explains.

"I set to work by establishing a team to look at the shifts. The next year, I communicated our transformation focus for PSA to our people, which included diversifying our business from primarily transshipment ports to a stronger focus on origin-destination ports and establishing our franchise value. It was not all smooth sailing

— there are always naysayers and people who prefer the status quo. But it is about inspiring the people around you with a shared vision of how we can perform and transform, building trust and affiliation so that people come along on the transformation journey."

THE MULTIDIMENSIONAL APPROACH TO BEING A SUPPLY CHAIN LEADER

"Head, heart, and guts — these are the three qualities a strong leader must have," Chong Meng says. On that first point: "It is important to be levelheaded, capable of connecting with everyone on the team. They should have the ability to share their vision and explain it so that others can understand."

Next, heart: "They should be able to engage with people authentically. They must inspire followership, trust, and spontaneous stretch instead of using commands to get the most out of others." And finally, guts: "The ability to make decisions and stand by them is a critical trait, especially amid the unknowns. A leader must be bold and capable of executing and handling strategic, people-oriented, and transformation issues."

Organizational transformation could be testing times for leadership, given that there is often no set rulebook to follow. For Chong Meng, such a moment came when he and others at PSA sought to enlighten the wider company about the growing importance of data and connectivity. "While it was not hard to convince people that the pace of change was accelerating in supply chains and warranted investment in technology, translating that into action was strenuous," he recalls.

Ultimately, PSA set up a core group called "B2B" — for "back to basics" — which met with Chong Meng every two weeks to devise and then drive initiatives that could offer value to the wider supply chain community. One such initiative involved engaging with beneficial cargo owners, who at that time lay outside of PSA's traditional group of customers. Chong Meng was instrumental in setting up PSA Cargo Solutions and securing a string of acquisitions such as CrimsonLogic and BDP International, which brought an understanding of customer-centric digitalization to the organization and also improved PSA's global supply chain capabilities.

"Leadership is about constantly ideating improvements in business and operations that can deliver a prosperous future to the organization," Chong Meng says, stressing that this principle applies to people as much as it does to processes: "Recruiting good people that fit this journey is vital. Given the complex nature of the supply chain roles being contemplated, I also look for some level of domain knowledge and experience as an important factor when recruiting for PSA."

SUSTAINABILITY AS A FUNCTIONAL NEED FOR THE FUTURE

Chong Meng is very pragmatic when contemplating the enormous task that confronts industry stakeholders in the mission to achieve net-zero carbon emissions. "As an industry, I feel we're ambitious with the claim of net-zero by 2050 without a proven roadmap as to how we would achieve it," he says. "We're looking at changing an entire system here, not just parts, so there's a lot of hard work and trade-offs."

As an example, Chong Meng cites the case of electric vehicles. Ironically, in the manufacturing stage, an electric vehicle actually has a heavier carbon footprint than a conventional vehicle; and further, if the electricity grids that power these cars are not drawing their energy from sustainable sources, then claim that electric vehicles are automatically more sustainable remains contentious. "Electric vehicles might look clean, but there are so many ways they can set you back before pushing you forward," Chong Meng says. "Charging infrastructure and smart usage are critical, for instance.

Everything has a bit of a trade-off that needs to be handled, and sustainability is no different.

"As a company, our first goal is to retain our license to operate by reducing our emissions within permissible limits. We have a plan in place for that. Beyond our own operations, we are also striving to help our customers and suppliers mitigate their carbon emissions."

With so many supply chain vendors in the mix, it makes sense for PSA to scrutinize its carbon mitigation strategies in order to derive a future competitive advantage from them. Understanding lower-tier emissions will help PSA rationalize strategies to push the company toward its net-zero goals. One of the focal points is the terminals, which Chong Meng claims are on the path to becoming a renewable net energy producer, rather than a consumer.

"I have reasons to consider our sea-facing ports as a place to generate power. A few well-planted wind turbines can power an entire port," he says. "I'm optimistic about enabling a greener supply chain. We are involved in many supply chain segments — ports, inland container depots, and container freight station services — and we want to shine the light on the end-to-end supply chain first to help the industry understand it. We then want to offer solutions for change."

Chong Meng stresses the need for the industry to understand the science, standards, and regulations governing sustainability in order to develop rigorous solutions that can be audited and scaled. PSA creates appropriate learning materials for its staff and participates in cross-industry forums, encouraging stakeholders to collaborate and share data on meaningful industry-wide use cases so as to move the needle collectively. "It's an inspiring journey, assisting people to be more innovative by opening their minds and stretching themselves," Chong Meng says. "Mere speech is not enough: you need to encourage them to be involved in things. That's how you build a greater capacity to change the world."

Chong Meng expresses the view that it is the sustainability agenda that will draw the younger generation into every industry, including supply chains. "The older generation that now heads supply chains did not hear of sustainability while growing up, while today's youth are different. Disruptions like the pandemic will fade from the limelight, but sustainability advocacy will continue to be in the news. Everything from real estate to industrial systems to supply chains needs to be reconfigured around sustainability. There is real scope to make a difference for sustainability through supply chain innovation, as the supply chain is so fundamental and pervasive in economic and social activities."

THE CONSCIOUS DECISIONS THAT CONTRIBUTE TO A STELLAR WORK CULTURE

To Chong Meng, leadership is about stewardship. "I feel very strongly that I have a responsibility to the people I lead. Stewardship is about being focused on the future, on what is beyond the present, and on building affiliations of trust so that my leadership team works well together and our people can thrive in their endeavors."

When people within an organization trust each other and subscribe to a shared vision, it creates a thriving, high-performance culture, which makes it easy for leaders to keep the company on course. Chong Meng attests that culture is born from regular investments in building trust and affiliation, forming a shared understanding of the world around the company and its role within it.

> "Stewardship is about being focused on the future, on what is beyond the present, and on building affiliations of trust."

"On a practical and daily basis, this translates into being mindful about empowering my leadership team and our people to determine what steps we need to take to realize our shared aspirations for the future" he says. "For me, this means I ask myself questions like, 'How do I create the space for people to engage in the next set of transformative discussions as an organization?' I address the 'why' a lot, making the conscious effort to always examine the future and not be too caught up in the present."

It's for this reason that Chong Meng finds value in systems thinking, which helps break down mental or operational boundaries and synthesizes the relationships between interconnected parts to reveal the impact this could have on supply chains and the business. "Importantly, it is about clarifying our shared values and actions, bringing people along the journey, addressing both hearts and minds," Chong Meng says.

Communication that touches the heart is critical, as motivated people within organizations can work against seemingly insurmountable odds. During an early-career posting to China, Chong Meng was faced with a situation that called for more than just good planning and tough calls: "It required people to have unshakable faith in the leadership and the decisions made." At that moment, Chong Meng recalled a line from the Chinese literary classic *Romance of the Three Kingdoms* uttered by the famed war strategist Zhuge Liang: "'Everything is ready, except for the East Wind,' said Zhuge Liang — it meant we had done all we could, and if we had faith in our choices, we needed to wait for the wind to change, and we could turn the disastrous situation into a winning one," Chong Meng recalls. "It is a saying that urges people to dig deep in the most difficult times. I used this line, and my Chinese team immediately understood what I meant, because they grew up hearing that story."

What followed was an amazing turnaround, as the team tapped into a deep vein of pride and emotion and threw themselves into the task at hand. "The experience showed me that leadership requires good decision-making, paired with the nurturing of strong affiliations amongst a team, so that we can prepare while we wait to catch our

East Wind, even when times are tough," Chong Meng says.

A high-performing team and culture will also create space for positive surprises. When there is a shared understanding of the "why" within an organization, the goal of a leader should be to create an expanded conversation, bringing in more leaders to work together as a team and have them think ahead in order to anticipate strategic shifts that the company needs to make. "I don't think I need to determine every path or choice ahead for us. Rather, I hope to motivate my leaders to take personal ownership of the steps we will take to co-create our future and that of our customers and stakeholders," Chong Meng says.

NURTURING INNOVATION AND ADOPTING TECHNOLOGY FOR IMPROVED OPERATIONS

For an organization like PSA, with its flagship operations at the epicenter of Singapore's trade network, technology remains a lifeline that expands the region's superiority in global maritime affairs. Chong Meng explains that Singapore's success as a global trade hub is due to its success at an ecosystem level. With over 160,000 people working across the city-state's maritime sector, the industry also has links to segments like finance, insurance, engineering, and government administration.

Singapore's government has taken the lead in building strong private-public partnerships that create value and move the needle on complex problems like decarbonization, data governance, and the deployment of new technology. In line with this, PSA has worked hard to solve supply chain pain points with efficient operations and continuous innovation. A notable example is PSA's speed of technology adoption. Since 1972, the organization has enacted and employed four generations of technology adoption at PSA Singapore's container terminals, which is particularly evident in the changes in yard cranes, quay cranes, and prime movers. While first-generation yard and quay cranes were operated manually, they underwent rapid automation at the turn of the 21st century.

"The second generation, brought in by 2000, saw our first trial of yard cranes having remote operators," Chong Meng says. "The third generation was ushered in in 2015, where we had fully automated yard cranes at Pasir Panjang, with remote operators stepping in only if necessary. The fourth and current generation is in the works, with the Tuas Port about to become the world's largest fully automated terminal, with unmanned electric automated guided vehicles (AGVs) and even quay cranes controlled remotely."

But these technological upgrades are only made possible by PSA's staff. Chong Meng points out that for each tech evolution, many PSA workers had to shift to the next-generation terminal and accustom themselves to working with different machines or systems, as well as acclimatizing to a changed work environment and new colleagues. "Some of these people are in their forties and fifties, handling containers in a certain way that they were used to for years. Making the transition required people to have a willingness to accept the need for change and to take steps to manage change — something that can only be possible if there is trust and a shared implicit understanding of the future," Chong Meng says. "At PSA, we make sure to build strong union–management relationships so that the entire team understands the 'why' of the change, and how this strong relationship supports our ability to ensure greater resilience for both the organization, and Singapore at large."

Scan the QR code below or visit www.sourcetosold.com to access exclusive bonus content you can use with your teams to further explore the concepts and insights covered in this book.

CHAPTER 14:

SASCHA MENGES

"The best leader would make himself or herself
unnecessary and fully replaceable."

Sascha Menges is the CEO of German industrial tool and hardware manufacturer Festool/TTS Tooltechnic, a position he took on in October 2021. He joined TTS after fourteen years with Stockholm-headquartered Husqvarna Group, where he led the Husqvarna Forest & Garden and Gardena division after having headed up their global operations for power equipment for forest, park and garden care. Prior to Husqvarna, Menges spent eight years as a consultant in the automotive and consumer goods divisions of McKinsey & Company.

Before his entry into the supply chain field, Sascha Menges pursued a career on the stage — in magic. "I used to do magic as a teenager, performing with a good friend of mine in many places — having a lot of fun practicing and performing," he recalls. And while his magician days are now well in the rearview mirror, Menges identifies some affinities between his former and current professions.

"Supply chain management is about driving change and communication," he says. "Specifically, if you run larger projects, you want people to change the way they see progress. Being comfortable with convincing and leading people toward your vision is important. Magic, being about both distraction and drawing attention to what you want people to see, can be an amusing parallel. I believe the presentation skills I honed while doing magic taught me how to feel comfortable on stage and keep people engaged."

Menges began his university studies in electrical engineering, but right from the beginning he had cross-disciplinary interests. "I was enrolled in TU Munich at that time, but I was always clear [that I wanted to move] to another city. So when ETH Zurich offered me industrial management along with my electrical degree, I decided to swap and move to Zurich.

"I found it intriguing to do a mix of science, engineering, and business. You do two years of pure engineering, followed by management, accounting and the like. It also landed me an internship at McKinsey & Company where I worked on trade brands in German food retailing, giving me great opportunities to develop beyond what I had studied in university thus far."

This internship led to Menges obtaining a permanent job in McKinsey's consumer goods sector after graduation. His next major career transition arrived when he consulted on a supply chain management project involving a two-week diagnostic with garden equipment manufacturer Gardena. "That was a point in my career where I had to decide on wanting to stay in consulting all my life or make a switch. I decided to switch, and fortunately it turned out good for me."

SCM AS A GATEWAY TO GENERAL MANAGEMENT

For Menges, there is no better way to segue into general management than by rising through the ranks in supply chain management. "One of the joys I had in managing supply chain operations is working on various projects and interacting with all sorts of stakeholders. SCM is the lifeline of several companies, and there's no success in the business if the supply chains don't work — as is clear from the disruptions caused by the pandemic, destabilizing operations around the world."

While there are many routes to climbing the ladder in general management, Menges argues that supply chain leaders have an edge as they intuitively understand how the underlying business works. "If you're in the supply chain, you understand many functions, you've worked with all of them, which eventually equips you to be responsible for all of them if you are elected to the top," he says. Furthermore, by being on the ground and witnessing the constant changes in day-to-day operations, SCM becomes something of a crystal ball that allows a glimpse of what the company will be facing in the future — an invaluable asset for anyone looking to move into the C-suite.

Regarding moving up in an organization, Sascha emphasizes the need to stay visible to top management. "They need to know your capability and trust your integrity, which, in essence, is the cause for any promotion. It's also important you make sure people understand that you can do more than what you're assigned to do — seeking stretch assignments and performing well in them helps."

However, becoming familiar to top management is no easy task, especially for those in SCM. "Being a supply chain professional, you are probably less loud and less demanding than some of the other functions like product management or sales," Menges observes. "For instance, you might be on the production side of the supply chain, which is typically a place where the top management does not travel, as factories are present in far-flung regions. This makes it that much harder for your effort to become visible to the management."

That lack of visibility is all the more regrettable given the fact that incorporating ground-level change within a company usually falls on the shoulders of SCM leaders. "The reality in SCM is that a lot of it is about driving change and bettering communication channels," Menges says. "If you're running larger projects, you want people to improve the way they forecast, produce, and even see change in the organization. Being able to feel comfortable at the helm and also convincing people to follow your lead is critical.

"Change management needs attention, as you'll have people who like change, people who follow you, and people who will resist the change," he continues. "A leader must learn to identify the people who resist, so that they can either pull them along, deploy them elsewhere, or get rid of them if they don't align with the company's ideals any longer. Driving change is a process, and SCM is all about that."

In Menges' experience, "change has been hardest with factory managers in lean transformations. For some, lean manufacturing may make their roles look more like standard operating procedures, rather than it being the art and science they've chosen to believe it is over the years. That said, people in the tier below — the factory workers — were clearly welcoming of lean, as they could voice their opinions and felt they were part of the improvement cycle. Once you have that grassroots support, managers will have to fall in line."

IMPLEMENTING LEAN MANAGEMENT INTO OPERATIONS

Menges' experience with lean management began right at the start of his stint in Gardena, fresh off being a consultant at McKinsey. "One of the first projects we undertook was to consolidate all the local warehouses across Europe into a few regional centers, to eventually create one consolidated European warehouse in Germany," he relates. "The decision was an easy one, considering the huge savings we were to make with the consolidation and the outlook of improved stock availability, which is so key to the seasonal nature of the Gardena business."

However, this transformation was inevitably met with some aggrievement from those Gardena employees in the international markets, who perceived that the consolidation would reduce the reliability of (and their influence over) operations in their regions. It was Menges' job to go around the regional warehouses, assuring these employees that the risk with the transition would be micromanaged and that they would not sit without stock. "I remember sitting with the regional heads and the salespeople as we closed a French warehouse, discussing what could go wrong and how to manage the risks associated with the closure," he says.

> "There's no one recipe for building trust — you just need to be transparent, don't hide your mistakes, and be involved in making things better for your people."

"Making people trust us that there's nothing better than storing all stock centrally, reducing the overall stock level and thus improving overall service level and availability, was harder than expected. They might have understood it conceptually, but they didn't trust it. Part of being a leader is being trusted, and if SCM is seen as biased toward one function or region, operations will not run smoothly. Ultimately, there's no one recipe for building trust — you just need to be transparent, don't hide your mistakes, and be involved in making things better for your people."

Gardena ended up creating test protocols before closing warehouses, which helped build credibility amongst the people in the regional markets. "Once we had the protocols running well, it was much easier to close the subsequent ones. The lesson was to ensure we don't choose the most difficult warehouse right at the beginning, but rather start with smaller but still relevant ones."

Gardena's acquisition by the Husqvarna Group in 2007 created new opportunities for Menges, as he now was part of a larger corporation that had several companies under its banner. Menges' new employers asked him to continue his supply chain management duties but expand them to a global level, entrusting him with the task of turning around operations for the company, which, at that time, was struggling to meet its commitments to customers.

"We had poor delivery services and too high inventory — all the things I had worked to streamline in the past for Gardena, by putting structures and systems in place," Menges recalls. Menges took on the challenge, implementing the lean management system across roughly twenty manufacturing units in the group. The new system helped reduce inconsistencies and injected flexibility into all aspects of operations, from sourcing and building inventory to even forecasting seasonality. "Rolling both challenges together — supply chain management and introducing lean management to our plant operations — turned out to be a productive combination," Menges says.

LEADERSHIP IS MORE THAN LEADING FROM THE FRONT

"The best leader would make himself or herself unnecessary and fully replaceable," Menges says. "This means that your subordinate can actually do everything that's needed operationally, and from a decision perspective you aren't needed. As a leader, if you could reach that state across your team — where you have people who can do the job better than you do — it means you have achieved great success."

As an SCM leader, achieving this state frees up time for you to think about operations more strategically, focusing on the long term rather than being bogged down by everyday workflows. "As a leader, you're expected to open doors for people and to make sure they have the right tools to do their job. You take care of the structures, ensure the team is built with a balance of the right capabilities needed to execute the strategy.

"I call this view of leadership 'lazy leadership,' but in a good sense. The aim is not to work hard yourself day and night, but build a great team and help them be productive and fly. People are averse to the idea of 'positive laziness,' but it is more of a reflection of the importance they place on being busy all the time. Personally, if

I'm busy 24/7 over weeks and months, I'd feel bad physically and mentally. It also shows that there's something wrong in the system if I'm measured by how busy I am, rather than how productive the operations turn out to be. The work-life balance is super-important. Life becomes so much more enjoyable that way."

Menges maintains that another crucial aspect of an SCM leader is the ability to stay curious. "I'm not much into books, but I stay curious about all kinds of business functions. I go to conferences and take meetings with like-minded people. You always learn something interesting. Curiosity is what got me here. When I started with lean management, I paired up with a great guy who was like my sensei. I asked him to train me, help me understand what we saw on the shop floor. Eventually, I learned a lot from him. It's critical to stay curious — you will pick up new things along the way."

In Menges' view, "supply chains are partly science and partly art. It's art because it is about the people: it takes skill and experience to understand the behavior and mindset of workers and to pick the right people to work together across functions. Ultimately, SCM is a people business. Driving change as a leader in the supply chain is all about the human element, and to me, that's the most interesting part of being in this line of business."

Scan the QR code below or visit www.sourcetosold.com to access exclusive bonus content you can use with your teams to further explore the concepts and insights covered in this book.

CHAPTER 15:

SAMI NAFFAKH

"As a leader, one of my key responsibilities is to anticipate volatility rather than react to it."

Sami Naffakh is the chief supply officer and a member of the group executive committee for Reckitt, a health, hygiene and nutrition products firm headquartered in the UK that he returned to in 2020 following a five-year tenure in internationally situated roles from 2003 to 2009. A twenty-five-year veteran of the fast-moving consumer goods (FMCG) industry, he has also held leadership roles with such major organizations as Unilever, Danone, and Estée Lauder.

To Sami Naffakh, one of the joys of working in the supply chain space has been the numerous international moves it necessitated for him. However, as Naffakh's wife has a phobia of flying, many of these relocations had to happen via road, rail, and boat — which, while manageable for relatively short-distance moves, took on the dimensions of an epic journey when Naffakh and his family had to relocate from the Netherlands to Singapore.

"It was a phenomenal and unforgettable family experience, and the nicest trip I've ever made," Naffakh remembers. "We rode all the way from France to Singapore by train, crossing Europe, Russia, China, and Southeast Asia. It took us six weeks to make the entire journey. We could have done it faster, but we stopped by, visited places, and connected with people on the route — it was good fun."

Clearly, Naffakh places great value on life experiences. "That's part of the fun of being part of supply chain management," he says. "I get to have opportunities to lead, engage, connect, and work across very diverse environments with people from different backgrounds."

Under pandemic conditions, of course, Naffakh had to assign the "fun" aspect of these interpersonal relations to the back seat while still making sure to create an atmosphere of trust. "In remote working conditions, establishing psychological safety within the workplace takes a lot longer. I see that within my team," he says. "As you don't often meet physically and only interact with people via a screen, building trust and bonding gets a lot more difficult. In a high-pressure remote working scenario, anything negative easily amplifies. Creating trust and providing a positive work experience is harder through digital interaction."

TEAM DYNAMICS ARE INSTRUMENTAL TO RUNNING AN EFFICIENT BUSINESS

"When there's true psychological safety at the workplace, people are more inclined to be their true self," Naffakh says. "They feel encouraged to speak their mind and, generally, feel more empowered. This is the best outcome, both for the individual and for the team."

In Naffakh's case, he had to overcome some of his own preconceptions about leadership to learn this lesson. After leaving Danone for Estée Lauder, he says that "I was a bit disoriented by the amount of time the then-executive vice president for supply chain was [allocating] for discussions and debates. It took me a while to understand that this wasn't a lack of drive or decisiveness [on his part], but a willingness to get all facts, views, contradictions, and tensions expressed before we made a critical decision. I soon realized how powerful this was in driving individual engagement and positive team dynamics."

However, leadership is also about coaching and guiding subordinates even while empowering them to express themselves. Attesting that he had no prior experience in leading large-scale industrial operations in multiple sites spanning many different countries when he was hired to do just this at Danone, Naffakh remembers that "the head of operations, rather than directing me, let me find my way, giving guidance whenever I asked for it and helping me reflect and learn from the mistakes I made along the journey."

Building a high-performing team involves a nuanced form of leadership that can foster deep chemistry between individuals, allowing them to bond over a common set of values and aspirations. Naffakh explains that the first step to this lies in selecting the right team. "Like a recipe, it all starts with the ingredients. Although skills and experience are undoubtedly important, I pay more attention to the value set, the cultural fit, the leadership skills, and the learning agility."

The next step is to help foster an environment in which the potential rapport between the various team members can flourish within the guardrails necessary for achieving business success. "There are two sides to leadership," Naffakh declares. "One is about clear governance, providing a set of rules and ways of working that everyone in the team adheres to and is eager to continuously improve.

"The other is about creating relationships — getting people to know each other, building respect and trust, and, finally, truly enjoying working together. Internal debates [in this climate] aren't perceived as aggression, but as a source of satisfaction. A team that enjoys being together will stand with each other when the journey gets challenging."

Another aspect of leadership is convincing peers and directing subordinates to execute the company's vision. When Naffakh joined Estée Lauder in 2014, the company's EMEA supply team was split between three locations: Belgium, the UK, and Switzerland. While the geographical dispersion was not an issue in itself, it quickly became apparent that the fact that each regional team was operating in a silo — each with its own organization, processes, and tools, and with limited collaboration and cross-fertilization — was adversely impacting performance, and was also a barrier to improvements.

Surveying this problem, Naffakh concluded that "consolidating the team and bringing it under one roof was the quickest way to address these gaps while also jump-starting the development of new capabilities and strengthening the talent bench. Nonetheless, everyone was far from being convinced to begin with, as there were significant concerns related to the material risk of losing a large proportion of incumbents. While this created an obvious risk of disruption in the short term, due to the loss of knowledge and experience, it also aroused wider concerns in a company that rightfully prides itself for caring about its people."

Estée Lauder took a twofold approach to this situation, Naffakh relates. First, the company emphasized the aims behind the transformation and the expected benefits for the company at large, particularly in regards to the strategic horizon, and how this fit with the overall business transformation journey. Secondly, management carefully listened to and addressed all the concerns raised, particularly from those who had spent a long time in the company, hence building confidence in the plans.

SUPPLY CHAIN RESILIENCY HELPS COMPANIES IMPROVE CONTROL OVER OPERATIONS

"The supply chain is a large set of operations and processes aimed at ensuring goods are made available to consumers at the right location, on time, at the right quality, and the right cost," Naffakh says. "To illustrate the importance of these functions — and how rarely they are truly comprehended and appreciated by those who depend on them — he offers an analogy: "If a company selling merchandise is a car, then its supply chain operations would be its engine. It sits under the bonnet so people cannot see it, and it is highly complex, so most people don't understand it."

However, Naffakh opines that "I think the pandemic has helped drive a better understanding of how vital supply is and how complex planning logistics operations can get. Consumers now realize it is critical, and that there's no such thing as unlimited capacity within supply chains. Even within companies, I see more appetite from the sales and marketing departments to look beyond their targets and choose to work around challenges plaguing sourcing and distribution networks."

Yet even as companies seem to be taking logistics concerns more seriously today, Naffakh remains cautious about their real commitment to creating resiliency and allocating the resources needed to future-proof their businesses against volatility. "When you overly depend on global trade, you are at risk of disruptions, be it geopolitical pressure or a pandemic. At the same time, there's still some skepticism about embracing transformation to drive up efficiency and visibility metrics. There's a disconnect between long-term and short-term expectations set by the market at large."

That said, pivoting firmly established operations and workflows is easier said than done —particularly for larger businesses, which, Naffakh contends, are generally slow in making decisions, making for a significant headwind when facing volatility. "This wasn't the case with Arla Foods, though," he notes, recalling another of his previous employment experiences. "One of the strengths of Arla was their cooperative model at scale, where they owned their entire supply chain — right from collecting milk at the farms to it finally ending up as products at the supermarket. Vertically integrating your supply chain can help give better control and leverage over operations."

No matter the size of the company, Naffakh encourages businesses to own a part of their supply chain so that they can create certain competitive advantages. "I'm not a fan of people who call for out-sourcing a company's entire logistics operation. There are many efficiencies to be gained from optimizing supply chains, from either a service or a cost standpoint. Companies must ponder if they can acquire the capabilities in-house or need to rely on an external partner to work it out. Logistics operations are now a differentiator and no longer just a cost center."

LEARNING COMES IN ALL SHAPES AND SIZES

"As a leader, one of my key responsibilities is to anticipate volatility rather than react to it," Naffakh declares, even as he notes that while keeping abreast of what is happening in the industry is critical for any executive, it can quickly drop progressively lower on their priority list given their hectic daily schedules. For his own part, "I keep myself updated primarily by reading. It's probably a generational thing, but I believe reading, by nature, allows more reflection than other types of media.

"I spend a fair amount of time reading the international press, as most events and developing trends have a significant impact on global supply chains. I also read the financial press, analyst reports, and financial reports, as it is a good way to get a grasp on how the competitive landscape is evolving."

On the interpersonal front, while Naffakh is not particularly fond of big conferences, he appreciates peer connections in small groups on specific topics, and also makes a point of interacting with external parties, including consultancy partners, analysts, suppliers, and service providers. Additionally, Reckitt organizes a number of network sessions for thought leaders and industry experts to meet, mingle, and hopefully create new perspectives. "I keep saying that in the wider supply chain community skills don't matter as much as before, as the volatile world we live in ensures the skills of today aren't the skills of tomorrow," Naffakh says. "What really matters is the ability to learn from people at all levels and to never stop learning at any point in your career."

While reading and spending time getting to know his peers in the industry has been an important part of Naffakh's success, experience — especially that gleaned from being in the eye of the storm — has been equally crucial, if not more so. "My first professional expatriation was when I was appointed factory manager in the UK [for Unilever]," Naffakh remembers. "It was my first large-scale management role, happening amid personal turmoil and on the back of an ambitious reorganization in the company. Plus, I made many beginner's mistakes, which made it even more complicated.

"The first step was for me to recognize and accept that I was on a bad course, and ask for feedback from my professional and personal circles. Unbiased feedback with a positive intent helped support and guide me, making a huge difference. Tough experiences also make up for a great learning experience."

> "As perceptions change, there's more realization that the supply chain is not just critical, but also gives a real competitive advantage — or disadvantage."

The sum of all that experience and learning has given Naffakh a clear-eyed appreciation for the centrality of the supply chain in the functioning of any business. "There are no sales activated or innovation plans materialized if the products are not hitting the shelves on time, in full, and at the desired quality. There is little chance of delivering any financial plan without working on the cost of goods sold and on the return on capital employed for the supply assets."

There are very few people, capabilities, and organizational projects that do not require intense involvement from the supply chain, which is where the majority of the workforce sits. Supply chain careers have a variety and diversity of options, giving endless opportunities to progress in the depth and breadth of one's skills.

"The clout of the supply chain is growing at the management board level within companies," Naffakh affirms. "As perceptions change, there's more realization that the supply chain is not just critical, but also gives a real competitive advantage — or disadvantage. Today, it's an exciting time to be part of the supply chain journey, simply because of its central role in ensuring the world continues to run in the way we know it."

Scan the QR code below or visit www.sourcetosold.com to access exclusive bonus content you can use with your teams to further explore the concepts and insights covered in this book.

CHAPTER 16:

THOMAS NETZER

"Leadership is also about adjusting the way you communicate [based on] the cultural environment you operate in. A leadership approach that works in North America may not work in Asia or Europe."

Thomas Netzer is the COO of the Boston-headquartered furniture and home goods e-commerce firm Wayfair, a role he accepted in 2019 after joining the year prior as the company COO and co-lead for Europe, where he was based out of Berlin. Prior to joining Wayfair he was a senior partner at McKinsey & Company for fifteen years, where he focused on the transportation and infrastructure industries and co-led McKinsey's global logistics practice.

Reflecting on his career development, Thomas Netzer looks back to the seven years he spent in India as a McKinsey partner as a key inflection point. "It came at a time when I was ready for a new challenge. I knew that working in a different country and navigating the many cultural differences and unique nuances of business interaction would present entirely new opportunities for my own personal development and growth as a leader," he says.

"I always liked looking at the big picture — trying something different, as long as it came with a lot of learning. Even if the move did not work out, I knew it would benefit me and let me grow from the experience. I had become set in my ways, and wanted to change that. The best way to do that would be to put myself in an environment where I had to stretch myself, an environment which was really outside my comfort zone. I narrowed it down to India, as I had never been there before, and it felt like a place that would make me rethink my perspective."

India lived up to his expectations. "When you're in a new country that's culturally completely different to where you're from, it's not as easy to strike up conversations and establish business relationships," he observes. "It's harder to find and establish a common ground and easy rapport.

"For instance, you have no idea how the Indian stock market functions, as you don't know the companies listed there. You can't connect over sports or politics, as there's no common ground there either. So for the first two years of being in India, I made sure I had an Indian partner with me every time I took a client meeting. This helped me break the ice with new business partners, create a safety net if needed, and establish a lot of credibility with my Indian partners, as they valued how much I valued them."

At the same time, local McKinsey associates remained skeptical about the "permanence" of Netzer's move, believing that he would only remain in India for a temporary stint. But as he invested time in working directly with the teams, the associates understood that he was in it for the long run, which changed their perceptions and helped Netzer gain people's trust across the company. This was one reason why Netzer was elected senior partner during his time in the country, the first time a non-Indian had ever attained this post.

Another reason for his success in India, Netzer says, was his understanding of the need for a flexible, adaptable leadership style. "I've realized leadership is also about adjusting the way you communicate to your subordinates, depending on the organization and the cultural environment you operate in. A leadership approach that works in North America may not work in Asia or Europe. You can be a straight shooter in a European setting, but in Asia, you've got to be subtle. You have to package instructions differently based on your surroundings, and understand the local culture and business norms."

This variability applies even to different sectors within the company, as leaders would have to apply different approaches to dealing with operations than they would when engaging with the development team. "You talk differently to your commercial stakeholder than your warehouse people. Context matters," Netzer says.

INFLECTION POINTS OF A CAREER IN LEADERSHIP

One of the lessons Netzer learned early on in his career was how to approach challenging operational problems. "I used to tackle problems by starting with a hypothesis of how to solve it, and then looking for data to prove the hypothesis. It is much more efficient to collect data to quantify the basis of a hypothesis," he asserts. "Unguided data collection carries the risk of boiling the ocean. This learning shaped the way I looked at business."

Another early learning came in the way he viewed entrepreneurship. "As an entrepreneur, you need to know everything happening within your business. You should develop client relationships, set the agenda, understand the business intuitively, and forecast bottlenecks. You need to know how to bring costs down while increasing revenue. Entrepreneurship unlocks a different way of thinking — a more holistic, more step-change-oriented way — which is quite different from being a manager," he says.

Across his career, Netzer has witnessed the impact that excellent hires have on an organization's health. "There are millions of smart and talented people out there, but the fundamental differentiator between the good and the greatest is commitment — whether people are really willing to go the extra mile," Netzer says. "When I look at people who are pivotal drivers of an organization, I take cognizance of not just their talent but also the commitment they bring to the table, because that makes a huge difference.

> "In soccer, you need to define your role in the team[;] it's
> the same within an organization — you must be clear on
> why you're there and what you're seeking to achieve."

"The more you go up the ranks, the more you need commitment. Money is an ingredient to commitment, but not the key. People are either intrinsically motivated and want to achieve something or they're not, and figuring that out is a huge driver for getting the right people into the business."

Being a soccer aficionado and coach, Netzer often makes analogies between soccer and business. "In soccer, you need to define your role in the team. You need to ask yourself if you're the striker, center midfield, or even the coach. It's the same within an organization — you must be clear on why you're there and what you're seeking to achieve."

But the parallels go even further than that, Netzer claims. "Having eleven players who are fit to take the field is not good enough. You need to have more players on the bench as backup, just in case someone gets injured," he says. "And as a coach, there's no way you can be on the pitch to score goals yourself. You will have to train the players to win games, and trust them. Be it a soccer field or a corporate environment, leadership is about putting the right people together, fostering interaction, and charging ahead as one well-oiled unit."

THE MAKINGS OF INTELLIGENT LEADERSHIP

"Independent of what you lead, you need to have certain leadership capabilities," Netzer stresses. "You must be able to create followership. To me, that's the most important indicator of a good leader — people will want to follow you. People will not just believe in what you do. You must be able to inspire, shape, and grow people, and make them believe they can have an impact working with you."

As part and parcel of this, he continues, leaders must stay away from micromanaging. Leadership is about providing subordinates with the right balance of coaching, guidance, and the freedom to make their own decisions. It is also vital to have a clear perspective of the company's goals, and be decisive about how to get there. "Communicating that perspective is critical to ensure the plan sticks with the whole organization. I believe it's even independent of the leadership role you have — if you don't develop clear plans and involve your people in the development, you will never get to where you want to," Netzer says. While simply having a plan is not a guarantee of success, by placing a premium on *communicating* that plan to the organization leaders can enable better alignment, which is crucial for successful execution.

Leadership is also about staying relatable to peers. When Netzer took up the job of COO at Wayfair, he had to move from Germany to Boston, with his family in tow. "I spent most of my first town hall meeting at Wayfair talking about my family and me, and why we came over. I didn't share content, just pictures. I showed the audience how I came to the US with my kids and a couple of dozen bags," he remembers. "I talked about the impact of moving continents with young kids in the family, and how challenging it was to transition them to a new school. I explained all of this to show them that I was there to stay for a long time, giving them a good reason to believe in me.

Another key attribute of leadership is honesty. Netzer speaks of how making mistakes is almost a certainty, especially in a consulting environment like McKinsey where critical decisions are an everyday affair. "In such situations, you have two ways to deal with it — you either defend your decision and create stories, or admit your mistake and correct it," he says.

One such experience came when a client tasked McKinsey with developing a digital strategy for them. "The project wasn't running on schedule, and three days before the final meeting, I figured out we did not have a digital framework in place, let alone a comprehensive strategy. In the end, we worked over a weekend and developed a document that looked great on the surface, but did not elaborate anything conclusive," Netzer relates.

"I requested a few more weeks to get the job done properly. The client was appreciative, admitting it to be a tough assignment. We did finalize a great strategy in the end, but this is one instance where people were willing to forgive and give me a second chance. Being open and realistic about a situation is always the right approach, even if the truth could be bitter sometimes."

MAINTAINING RELIABILITY IN THE WAKE OF SUPPLY CHAIN DISRUPTIONS

When COVID-19 became a full-blown pandemic, it brought entire global supply chains to a screeching halt as governments discussed what counted as "essential" logistics. For Wayfair, the question of the "essentiality" of the company's business was an understandably urgent one. "The issue was that while we were considered essential, a lot of our suppliers weren't," Netzer says. "But if that's the case, 80 percent of our supply would have vanished, as we only had about 20 percent of our inventories sitting at our warehouse.

"This led us to do all we could to avoid warehouse operations getting shut down. We explained to the relevant authorities that while it might not be essential for people to have a table in their house during the pandemic, the quarantining measures would mean many of them stay and work from home. And that would warrant a need for home furniture and equipment to keep them productive. This was a game-changing argument, as no one questioned the essentiality of our business after that."

For an e-commerce major like Wayfair, product availability is a priority. "It's the oxygen of our business," declares Netzer. "If I don't have products available, I don't have anything to sell. As a supply chain leader, creating that availability is crucial.

"The second thing you have to make sure of are speedy and reliable operations. If you are not fast enough in your consumer's eyes, you don't convert leads on your site. If you have a wonderful sofa that you deliver in two years, you can be sure no one puts that in their cart. On the flip side, if you can deliver it in three hours, but it's broken, or you promised to deliver it in three hours and it comes in three days, you are not reliable. The customer will never return to your website, so you can't build repeat patronage for your brand. Speed drives conversion and reliability creates repeat purchases, and supply chain leaders need to have a plan to execute that."

Aside from managing consumer expectations, companies must look to increase cost efficiency to improve their bottom lines. Netzer contends that he does not believe in incrementally improving cost position, but rather in radical changes that move levers to bring costs down. "The job of a supply chain leader is not an extension of the work managerial colleagues execute on a daily basis," he says. "As a leader, I shouldn't be hanging out in the warehouse telling workers how to improve forklift operating efficiencies. I have to trust that my warehousing managers can do that.

"Leaders should not be thinking of incremental progress, but of looking out for disruptive ideas. The constant push for innovation is, to me, one of the most rewarding parts of being in the supply chain."

Scan the QR code below or visit www.sourcetosold.com to access exclusive bonus content you can use with your teams to further explore the concepts and insights covered in this chapter.

CHAPTER 17:

ERNEST NICOLAS

"When I am inside the four walls of Rockwell Automation, I am accepted as a member of the executive leadership and the chief supply chain officer, but when I leave, I am a black man burdened with the weight of so many negative stereotypes of my demographic that so many people consume in the media."

Ernest Nicolas is senior vice president and chief supply chain officer at Rockwell Automation in Milwaukee, where he has overall responsibility for the integrated supply chain that plans, sources, makes and delivers Rockwell products and services to customers. He came to Rockwell in 2006 as a project manager and took on several roles of increased responsibility prior to his present position, including VP of global supply chain and SVP of operations and engineering services. Prior to his time at Rockwell, he held a number of supply chain, manufacturing engineering, and manufacturing operations positions with the General Motors Corporation.

As the chief supply chain officer of Rockwell Automation since the beginning of the COVID-19 pandemic, Ernest Nicolas has had a ringside view of the end-to-end integrated supply chain of an industrial company during a uniquely chaotic time for global supply chains. But as he tells it, the pandemic did have a silver lining. "Organizations that long maintained the very traditional view of their supply chain as merely an execution arm or just a cost-productivity engine learned firsthand through the pandemic that there are severe consequences for not steadily investing in a supply chain strategy rooted in agility and resilience," he asserts.

"I can clearly see that the pandemic is changing C-suite behavior in real time, as organizations rapidly adjust for the very dynamic and volatile business climate. People across the enterprise are learning more and more about the challenges faced by supply chain practitioners. Technology companies are mushrooming in the supply chain space to complement the areas [that have needed] improvement for a long time. We are in for a transformation that will take us on a significant journey over the next several years."

"When you add to that the everyday reality of the macroeconomic environment — be it geopolitical challenges or market constraints — all of that is forcing us into an environment where well-functioning supply chains can be a differentiator, with the ability to add significant value to organizations."

As the head of the supply chain at Rockwell, Nicolas is tasked with ramping up capabilities at a quick pace in an environment beset with procurement uncertainties, steep freight costs and labor shortages. "Building capability from the ground up involves improving technology, establishing physical capacity, and revamping business processes," he says. "Supply chain leadership is as tough a job as it is exciting. We are a meaningful part of the foundation of this company, and no longer an afterthought.

"Thanks to the pandemic, supply chain professionals are perceived differently in this market. While this has created its own set of unique challenges, it is very positive to see the perception change."

THE YIN AND YANG OF SUPPLY CHAIN COMPETENCIES

Nicolas contends that there are two sets of professionals operating at opposite ends of the spectrum within the supply chain department.

"[On one end] we've got the employees who go deep into the processes. They've mastered their core discipline, identifying themselves as the sourcing, logisticians, operations leaders, or supply chain planning people.

"On the other end, we've got people who are masters of supply chain orchestration. They've done multiple functions, from procurement, planning, and logistics to working in the factory on repair and manufacturing."

Nicolas explains that the orchestrators are the change agents, the early adopters who can envision new technologies and systems and thread them from one end of the supply chain to the other. The process- and discipline-focused workers, by contrast, are more rigid in their views. "They tend to be hesitant about integrating the supply chain given their depth of knowledge in a specific function. This is why the balance is so important," Nicolas explains.

> "Thinking about changes in every step, from design to
> product launch, is essential. Companies will have
> to actively dismantle siloed thinking processes that inhibit
> collaboration between various segments within the organization."

"We need both these groups: the deep experts, and the orchestrators working in concert to adapt to the changes. Organizations today lack a balance in representation of these groups. The right balance across these two groups allows for organizations to appropriately visualize the supply chains of tomorrow. Until we get people with an understanding of an integrated end-to-end supply chain into executive roles, we will continue to be challenged to work through sudden disruptions."

Change management, therefore, is critical. "Thinking about changes in every step, from design to product launch, is essential. Companies will have to actively dismantle silo-thinking processes that inhibit collaboration between various segments within the organization," Nicolas says. "This demands integrated thinking that goes beyond regular operations — like working to design supply resiliency, understanding the future regulatory environment, and [determining] how to position supply chains accordingly."

THE NEED FOR RESILIENCE IN SUPPLY CHAIN PLANNING

Whereas the 2011 Fukushima nuclear plant explosion caused only a minor disturbance to global supply chain functioning, the pandemic lasted long enough to create a tidal shift in how supply chains run. "The inflation caused by the pandemic seems very real," Nicolas observes. "Labor shortages are real, and these are major factors that impede companies like Rockwell Automation from leveraging our full capacity to build products. All of this comes into play and impacts the bottom line."

The pandemic has helped trigger a supply chain renaissance that has forced top management to sit up and take notice of potential threats that many companies had never truly considered. "I remember not being taken seriously when I presented enterprise risk strategies a decade ago," Nicolas says. "There was confidence in operations 'finding a way.' Many felt that there wouldn't be any challenges that would extend beyond a few weeks, and [would] be resolved by the end of the quarter. In support of this thought process, historically there were no supply chain challenges that were significant to categorize them as being an existential risk.

"But here we are, bringing back all the risk mitigation plans and pondering ways to quickly establish resiliency. The pandemic taught many executives to reconsider proven strategies of having significant portions of their manufacturing operations centered in a certain geographic location. Companies are [now] thinking of ways to protect their business from geopolitical risks and build resilience across different facilities. Thinking this way will drive companies to try some dramatically different strategies compared to what they've employed in the past."

To cite an example, one of Rockwell's issues during the pandemic was a shortage of electronic components, which hampered their ability to rapidly ramp up sales. "Everything happens in cycles. Today, companies are emotionally driven, frustrated at their inability to convert backlogs and take full advantage of the surging market," Nicolas opines. "Emotions shape the company's behavior, and when there's a market correction, we won't go back to where we started pre-pandemic. People are now more informed on what it means to run optimized supply chains, as they recognize that lean manufacturing — and not lean supply chain — is the right answer."

BUILDING THE SUPPLY CHAIN COMMUNITY OF TOMORROW

Nicolas is of the opinion that to build a network of able supply chain professionals, it pays for the community to start doing what engineers have done for ages: cultivate an analytical mindset that is sharpened through years of rigorous education. "Engineers do a full study, and focus on math and science to develop the mindset to solve engineering problems. The supply chain community should sit up and take notice."

Reflecting on his own entry into the field, Nicolas states that while supply chain is, in reality, very attractive as a profession, it continues to lack the comparative sheen of engineering. "As I look back on my own education, I was not very well aware of the true complexities of the integrated supply chain. I understood the meaning of the supply chain buzzwords: I understood fundamentally 'purchasing' was buying, 'planning' was scheduling, and 'logistics' was shipping and transportation. But when I looked at engineers, their work seemed much more attractive. It involved designing or creating products you can see in the market. There was a gratification to problem-solving.

"As I fast forward 25-plus years into my career, I can very easily say that supply chain work offers the same level of gratification, and clearly has its own sets of intricate challenges."

This is why educating people early on about what a career in supply chain actually entails is so important. "We have to pivot engineers to come work in this space. Due to societal pressure, individuals don't always know what they want to do, and naturally shy away from production, operations, and supply chain management. I didn't consider supply chain a viable career when I started, but had I known then what I do now, I would have chosen to focus on it sooner."

Nicolas contends that the key is to introduce people to what is attractive about working in the supply chain. At Rockwell, he found himself in a situation where people in the organization approached the wrong department for their supply chain problems. "It drove me crazy, because I understood they were missing out on the complexities of what we do. I've spent a lot of time reminding people about the basic SCOR model — plan, source, make and deliver. The visibility this brings across various operational areas is important to me.

"Using this SCOR model, I highlight to them that the core functions are equally important from an execution perspective, with planning being the most critical step of them all. We buy what's planned, we make what's planned, and we ship what's planned. If you make mistakes in planning, you will be chasing products through the rest of the supply chain. Of course, it's more intricate than that, but at least it helps educate different organizational units on the overall process."

APPRECIATING ETHNIC DIVERSITY WITHIN SUPPLY CHAIN LEADERSHIP

"On a daily basis, I am challenged with finding balance in how I communicate as I work through being the 'only'. Most companies do not have many executives that look like me. What many fail to understand is that my experiences differ significantly at work versus when I leave work.

"When I am inside the four walls of Rockwell Automation, I am accepted as a member of the executive leadership and the chief supply chain officer, but when I leave, I am a black man burdened with the weight of so many negative stereotypes of my demographic that so many people consume in the media.

"You have to keep in mind that these experiences aren't mutually exclusive. As I've matured, I have learned to live with it. It's challenging at times, and I'd be lying if I told you it was not."

Nonetheless, this pressure has only strengthened Nicolas' resolve to bring diversity to the board table. As part of this, he joined the Executive Leadership Council (ELC), an all-Black organization focused on executive pipelining. "They target Fortune 1000 executives that are two levels removed from the CEO," he explains. "They want individuals to inspire their organizations to pipeline the next generation of Black executives. They organize leadership programs at all levels, such as mid-level-managers symposiums, leadership weeks for directors, and C-suite academies to drive readiness for high-potential Black talent"

The crux of the ELC's efforts, Nicolas states, is its focus on learning from a Black person's perspective: "[The] sessions bring to light our experiences, [the] conscious and unconscious biases [we encounter], and the microaggressions [we face]." Inspired by his experiences with the ELC, Nicolas started a Black executive leaders group within Rockwell, for people at the director level and above. "We built it around the idea of camaraderie, because our individual challenges were quite niched when compared to the broader mass of the organization. We went from getting to know each other to establishing a mission and vision.

"Our focus has been to assist Rockwell Automation through the life cycle of our diverse employees. We actively participate in recruiting events, host mentoring sessions, and meet with our C-suite executives to discuss diversity, equity, and inclusion opportunities within the company."

Nicolas is proud of diversity and inclusion initiatives such as this, calling them a chance to help people achieve their career aspirations and find ways to be comfortable in environments that were not always built for them. "This initiative is near and dear to my heart, and I'm as passionate about it as I am about the supply chain. It's gratifying to be around a cause like that."

"If you look at my career trajectory, or that of any executive, someone [at some point] thought of giving us a chance. That's all anybody — especially the underrepresented — wants. A chance to be challenged. A chance to succeed. Many of the underrepresented don't know what they can do yet. Through intentional assignments into some very challenging situations and positions, Rockwell helped me stretch myself. Inclusivity makes organizations truly democratic, and personally, it would be great to see supply chains pick up the baton."

Scan the QR code below or visit www.sourcetosold.com to access exclusive bonus content you can use with your teams to further explore the concepts and insights covered in this book.

CHAPTER 18:

TOMMY NIELSEN

"I like challenging things; I think it's in my DNA."

Tommy Rahbek Nielsen is the EVP and COO of the Denmark-based Vestas Wind Systems A, where he is responsible for driving innovation and operational efficiency in the next phase of the global transition to sustainable energy. He has held a number of senior positions in his more than twenty-five years at Vestas, rising from finance manager to CFO for Vestas Central Europe, VP and managing director for China, and Group SVP for global supply chain planning.

"I like challenging things, to see progress, to develop people ... I also like tying the entire value chain together," says Tommy Nielsen, the COO of Vestas, a company he has been serving for 24 years now. Before he found his niche in the world of wind turbines, however, Nielsen spent nine years at a smaller company that built boilers and heating units for households.

"It was the kind of company where, if you passed nine or ten years, you'd probably end up being there for the next thirty-five years. While I was educated to be a normal bookkeeping assistant, I did start working on the factory side, as it interested me on how I could tie production together with IT and digitalization. And this is way back—in the late '80s, to be precise," Nielsen recalls.

Immediately after progressing from bookkeeping assistant to the role of chief accountant, Nielsen got a call from a headhunter asking if he was interested in hearing about a company in the area. "It was a strange call. He then faxed me a brief explainer on the proposed role to my main number at work. My secretary found the page in the fax machine, and I had actually declined to talk to this company," Nielsen says. "This was because I had just been promoted and wanted to stay on in my first leadership role, where I can serve the person who educated me during my traineeship."

But the headhunter was persistent, and after being approached for the fourth time Nielsen finally agreed to talk with the company. That company was Vestas, and Nielsen hasn't looked back since. "It took me six months to say yes, and I haven't regretted my decision," he says.

As soon as he arrived, Nielsen began noting those areas that were ripe for transformation. "When I joined Vestas, I immediately saw that we didn't have much control over the supply chain. This was because the idea back then was simple — sell whatever you produce. And we were growing at over 30 percent year on year, so we behaved like an entrepreneurial company and did not look to bring in a structure that's more reflective of a more established firm."

Stationed in Germany in the company's sales unit, where he was tasked with setting up workflows and sending out reports, Nielsen soon recognized an even greater problem in managing Vestas' operations. "We didn't know something as simple as what it cost to run the turbine. The way we were running our accounts, we didn't know if we would be making a profit till the end of the year. This is unpleasant — we went public in 1998, and we didn't know in the middle of the year how operations were going to pan out."

At that time, Vestas had reports scheduled every month that ran to thirty pages, which Nielsen had to prepare. After the first few months Nielsen realized that people were not engaging with the report, due to the exhaustive way it was structured. "While I was writing one such report, I suddenly decided to write random filler sentences in the middle of the report, counting on the fact that no one was actually paying attention. I had a good relationship with the CFO of the group at that point, and so I figured I would not be in a spot if I was caught in the act."

Nielsen's luck held for three months, until he finally got a call from the fuming CFO asking what was wrong with him. "And that was exactly the point," laughs Nielsen. "We were creating a lot of reports in the organization, and we didn't use them much. What was the point of it all? I like challenging things; I think it's in my DNA."

In some ways, Nielsen's foray into logistics was also a part of him challenging and exploring newer pastures. "I've always wanted to be a CFO, right from the moment I started my trainee job in 1988," he says. "At Vestas, I went back to Germany as CFO of Central Europe, at which point I was thinking of leaving the company. I spoke to another privately owned company in the area for a CFO position, but I realized I wouldn't have autonomy over decisions working in a family-controlled company. That's when I decided to stay on at Vestas and do something different from finance."

PUTTING STRUCTURES IN PLACE FOR QUALITY CONTROL

The turn of the century brought in an increased push for renewable energy, helping lift businesses like Vestas. Nielsen describes how this led the company to construct its supply chain from the ground up, including adding capacity by building factories.

"At this point in time, it was a rush to add capacity and not about the finances, as we were sure that we could sell whatever we produced. We knew we were making money, but didn't know to what extent. This was when we realized that it was not just about building the ecosystem, but also about being in control of the variables — for instance, exerting control over your supplier base."

In a heated market where demand outstrips supply, complacency can set in — a situation Nielsen navigated by introducing quality control into sourcing operations. This was not easy, considering the procurement division only focused on buying materials without expecting standardized quality across all vendors. "When there's heavy growth, controlling quality is hard," Nielsen says. "Back then, quality issues were commonplace. There are still quality issues in the industry, as it still isn't as mature as, say, the automotive industry. We took our employees into our confidence and clearly outlined what we wanted to achieve as a company. But it was hard for people to get used to the structures we put in place and to act on available data — they were so used to just acting on gut feelings."

The issue with this kind of intuitive approach, Nielsen argues, is that it remained siloed within a select few individuals in the company, which bogged down the system as scaling up was not easy within human-centric operations. It was clear that growing outside of Denmark and having seamless operations across the world was not possible with just a few people micromanaging everything at the top.

For his part, Nielsen brokered a deal with Vestas' suppliers from Germany and Denmark, calling on them to build their capacity in China and promising to pay for their investment over the first three years. "They had a fantastic deal. If you look at our supply base, it took us some effort and time to transition from a European-centric supply base to a Chinese-centric one.

"The journey needs faith. How do you trust the Chinese if you have the notion that Chinese products are of poor quality? This is a wrong perspective, but it makes clear the need for quality control. We took a lot of people from supply policy into Vestas at that time to ensure we could lift every vendor to the quality level we were expecting. Today, all the products we source are of the same specification and quality, be they from Europe or Asia."

INDUSTRY COLLABORATION IS THE NEED OF THE DAY

Nielsen contends that operations within the wind turbine industry will change quite drastically in the near future: "You'll see fewer big assembly lines, machines will be assembled at the site, and we are going to see turbines go off-grid." He also argues that, as sustainability as a cause continues to gain momentum worldwide, the interest that this creates in the wind turbine industry needs to be channeled efficiently.

"Looking at the next five years, we need to ensure the supply base is consolidated," Nielsen says. "We have too many small suppliers who will not be Tier 1 suppliers to companies like Vestas. We need suppliers with more muscle and an industrialized background, being part of a bigger group. The future will also see us pushing the assembly part of operations out of the company and relying on external firms. This is exactly why we need strong partners."

In addition to consolidation within the supply base, Nielsen also advocates for collaboration between industry stakeholders. "It is amazing to see the money that's being deployed into this space. It is up to us to take it or to lose it. To capture the opportunities, it is critical to have collaboration between major players. While we use the same supply base, we have businesses that are pointing in different directions. This is driving costs up, and not really helping the industry overall."

"Companies complain about how costs of doing business are rising, but they aren't actively working to circumvent that... it's essential to stay entrepreneurial if we are to see growth, but in a more structured and less dynamic way."

Nielsen has strong opinions on the topic of collaboration, which he sees as an existential need for the industry in order for it to scale efficiently. "My colleagues from other companies in the business are tight-lipped about sharing information on operations. I tell them that we have blades with similar size and dimension, similar sellers, and even similar transport equipment. If there's collaboration within the industry, it is possible to drive costs down."

Such a collaboration can help bring more transparency into the system. Visibility across the supply chain can be particularly beneficial given pandemic-induced sourcing issues, helping companies weather volatility and bring order into operations. "Why couldn't we foresee a pandemic or the Suez Canal accident? Shouldn't we be predicting the consequences by now?" Nielsen asks. "While we don't have answers to such questions, what we can do is learn from them every time and look to be more transparent with other supply chain stakeholders."

Considering the abundant opportunities within the industry, Nielsen declares that protectionism could be a problem in the post-pandemic environment. "Companies complain about how costs of doing business are rising, but they aren't actively working to circumvent that. I tell my colleagues that it's essential to stay entrepreneurial if we are to see growth, but in a more structured and less dynamic way."

BUILDING UP INDIVIDUALS TO CREATE A RESILIENT ORGANIZATION

Within an organization as well, Nielsen argues for the importance of collaboration and regular infusions of new ideas and personnel with different skill sets. "I spend considerable time with my leadership team brainstorming on how to develop talent both from the inside while also getting energy from outside," he says. "[For example, a couple of years ago] I was a bit burned out running assembly lines, and was finding myself short of ideas. I realized we needed energy from outside, and so we started hiring from different industries, including the auto segment.

"It is always about getting together the right team with the right skill set at the right time. We hired a new CTO in 2020, during the height of the pandemic, who came with more than twenty-five years of experience [in the trucking industry]. He's perfect for us now, but had we taken him in eight years ago, it would probably have been too early in our evolution as a company [for us to get the most out of him]."

Nielsen explains that the kind of people he looks for are the ones that are ready to go beyond what they have learned and dare to step out and "test the waters from time to time." "Encouraging young people is key," he states. "I look back at my own career, and every time I was thrown in deep water, I survived — that's why I sit here today. The other day, we discussed promoting a thirty-two-year-old woman to a leadership position, which was met with some skepticism — some people thought she was too young for the role. Then we looked around the room, and realized that each one of us would have been scandalized if we were told we were too young to step up when *we* were thirty-two!"

Creating a culture within the organization is also central to a business' health. In Nielsen's case, "I'm trying to create a culture around customer focus. This needs to be driven to the farthest end of the supply chain, as the company will become an island if they lose focus on what the customer needs. This means that operations and supply chain teams must connect and work closely with the sales and marketing teams to ensure synergy."

Standing at the helm of logistics for a multibillion-dollar company, Nielsen observes that supply chain management is fuel for the future rather than a cost center. "Coming from finance, I thought that supply chain was not really where things were happening; but today, I can see that it's the glue holding a company together. We have to engage with universities and tap into young talent by coming out and telling them success stories from the industry. As supply chain leaders, we must ensure we bring in enough trainees to keep scaling our ecosystem."

Scan the QR code below or visit www.sourcetosold.com to access exclusive bonus content you can use with your teams to further explore the concepts and insights covered in this chapter.

CHAPTER 19:

BEATRIX PRAECEPTOR

"A high-performing supply chain is not so much about processes and tools as about people collaborating and communicating effectively."

Beatrix Praeceptor is the chief procurement officer of the UK-listed paper and packaging company Mondi Group, based in Vienna. She began her career at the consumer electronics manufacturer Phillips Industries, where she worked for nearly eight years before moving to the French building materials supplier Lafarge S.A. as their logistics manager and, subsequently, SVP supply chain manager, before moving to Mondi in 2011.

While so many professionals today have carefully structured their career roadmaps, Beatrix Praeceptor's career in supply chain came about through happenstance. "I began my career at Philips because I thought it would give me the perfect avenue to use the language skills I picked up when I was young," she says. "I also wanted to aim higher, and [since Philips was] an international company rather than a local, Austrian one, it felt right."

Praeceptor started in procurement, which was her doorway to the industry that's been her home for over three decades. "While in procurement, I found the magnitude of the end-to-end supply chain fascinating. I understood that being a supply chain manager gave you control over the entire value chain, irrespective of what you produced."

When she moved from Philips to building materials major Lafarge, she developed a passionate determination to make a difference in their logistics operations. "I quickly realized that if I wanted substantial improvement, I had to go the extra mile and optimize every step and interface along the way," she recalls.

"We were frequently running out of products, and I had to develop a solution to this problem. As a supply chain manager, locating exactly where the problem lies is much like a spider closing in on an insect in its web. You might be sitting at the top of the pyramid, but it's imperative you see the whole picture and sense the problems downstream. This helps you analyze the problem better and react to it in the best way possible."

Praeceptor's experience as a supply chain manager has helped her grasp the importance of sales and operations planning in running a seamless supply chain. "I could see that a high-performing supply chain is not so much about processes and tools as about people collaborating and communicating effectively. [So] I gathered people with the right skill sets, a collaborative mindset, and holistic thinking around the table to ensure [we] have the system up and running [as it should].

"Whatever the situation, I found myself constantly thinking of the supply chain angle to processes. One of the biggest learnings I've had is that different functions and departments within an organization work in silos, but [these] have their limits. The pandemic years have especially underscored the interdependencies along the supply chain and how collaborative thinking is now imperative. You have to think and work with an end-to-end mindset and by collaborating with others to keep the systems running smoothly."

COLLABORATION IS KEY FOR SUPPLY CHAINS OF THE FUTURE

Praeceptor observes that supply chains are transitioning from an environment in which they were purely transactional to a more collaborative, support-oriented structure. "Now, you need to bring data, people, and topics together to make supply chains work. It's about building networks. There's a constant need to ensure people and data collaborate across the value chain.

"You need to ensure that the customer understands your suppliers' constraints. A few years ago customers wouldn't be interested in such information, but it's necessary to understand the different elements of a business in a world that is more and more connected. This helps to make accurate decisions."

For Praeceptor, viewing supply chains through the lens of procurement when she entered the field allowed her to appreciate the fact that the industry was not all black or white. "We rarely have a single root cause when something goes wrong. If we don't have the raw materials, it might not be the supplier's fault or inefficient tracking of goods. There can be multiple reasons — from demand being higher than expected, to closed ports, to other macroeconomic factors out of our control, like COVID-19 or the US–China trade war. These reasons queue up to create a massive bottleneck, bringing the industry to a standstill."

> "I believe the transactional aspect of a business must be left to machines and artificial intelligence. We as human beings should provide value by building relationships."

In Praeceptor's view, building solid data networks and fostering partner relationships is critical for risk mitigation, given the volatility that has become a norm today. "Anyone who understands this has the edge over their competition," she says. "Disruptions will continue, and a collaborative network will help you operate faster and better. I believe the transactional aspect of a business must be left to machines and artificial intelligence. We as human beings should provide value by building relationships."

At Mondi, Praeceptor's role involves working closely with her stakeholders to mitigate their risks. "We maintain several plants where we can get the product out and update our customers with accurate information early on, especially when we know that there will be a problem down the line. We inform them when we understand that we won't [be able to] fulfill an order because we're running short of raw materials."

Building reliable relationships with vendors and customers ensures that the company can handle its day-to-day operations smoothly while maintaining transparency and open communication. Great relationships built during the best of times will be a lifeline when crisis strikes, which Praeceptor cites as a valuable lesson that she learned in the pandemic years.

"Companies abusing the situation to increase their margins forget that things will change someday, and they need to balance. Everybody understands that you need to grab opportunities when running a business, but it needs to be done in a way where you also keep your relationships. That's where strategic supply chain thinking comes in.

"With the right relationships in place, you work with people to brainstorm the risks and mitigate them. Maybe nine out of the ten ideas you come up with will never apply, but even if one of them does, you'll build an edge over your competitors."

While the structural issues that the pandemic laid bare have pushed some companies to seriously consider turning to regional supply chains rather than continuing to pursue a globalized model, Praeceptor refuses to get behind this idea. "While scaling back on the extent of globalization seems inevitable, companies need to build a better mix of regional, local and global networks. This will, of course, have good and bad aspects to it.

"The good part is that such strategies will help [us] focus more on local economies and reduce our dependence on global sourcing. But localization can be a hassle for smaller companies that do not possess the resources to invest close to home, resulting in them struggling to adapt."

STRENGTHENING SUPPLY CHAINS THROUGH PEOPLE MANAGEMENT

"When you're in supply chain, you need to be able to juggle more balls in the air than in many other functions," declares Praeceptor, contending that most people in management would have great difficulty dealing with the complexity that supply chain entails. Being forced to deal with so many different aspects of a process amid a lot of ambiguity is uniquely taxing, and Praeceptor reckons that finding people capable of managing complex information within an intricate network is the biggest challenge facing supply chains today.

"We need to have more social skills to build our networks. That's something I have a bird's-eye view of from a leadership perspective," Praeceptor says. "That being said, the next generation of people eager to move into the supply chain looks promising. They understand that when it comes to aspects like sustainability, it is within the supply chain where you can make a real difference.

"For a prospective supply chain leader, sourcing products, dealing with suppliers, and doing end-to-end business must sound exciting. So should the idea of processing various information flows and managing a complex supply chain. They should know that if they want to significantly impact the company's bottom line, there's no better division to work in than the supply chain."

Praeceptor now teaches in the sustainability area at the Fachhochschule Wien (the Austrian equivalent of an applied sciences university) to help foster the next generation of supply chain leaders by bringing a practical perspective to education. She explains that supply chains are more about common sense than theory, as real-time operations demand finding solutions to problems that seldom find their way into textbooks. "How do you analyze an issue? Who do you approach when you have an issue? How do you get the people involved to talk to each other? Understanding the big picture from the beginning to the end and the implications of your actions along the value chain is vital," she says.

"I remember an issue at Lafarge, where one of the more challenging tasks was to get the production manager, sales manager, procurement manager, and dispatch manager in a room and make them agree on a common solution. This is one of the trickiest parts of working in a live supply chain scenario that they don't teach in universities. Everybody has their competencies, but you need to build trust to make the whole story work together rather than solve the problem on your own."

Praeceptor is a firm believer in the value of experience, especially in top leadership, where she contends that it helps foster the kind of agile mindset that comes in handy when responding to problems. "Experience teaches you to overcome things and always have a way out of situations," she says. "When you're young, any crisis makes you think that the world will crash. But once you've seen a bit of the world, you understand that these things happen, and you'll survive. As a leader and a person of experience in the industry, it's your job to keep your people calm — especially in crises, when people [often] can't think or act straight. You can use your experience to make them believe that they'll overcome the situation."

PERSUASION AS A MEANS TO THE END

Praeceptor explains that it is critical to make people understand where they stand relative to the value chain at large. "If you need people to collaborate with you, you need to show them the bigger picture. If you show someone the before-and-after picture of the impact, you can convince them of your way of thinking. If we can develop a way of thinking [that is] aligned across the board, we can work toward a common outcome that benefits both our internal processes and the customers."

In Praeceptor's opinion, the four essential elements a team needs to have are trust, conflict capability, accountability, and common targets. On that first point, she stresses the importance of leaders putting in the necessary effort to truly win the confidence of the people they're working with. "Building this foundation of trust is the most difficult part of this equation, especially with people who are not a direct part of your team," she says. "With that, the rest of the things follow." For Praeceptor, the path to trust involves a twist on the concept of the *Golden Rule*. "The easiest way to keep people motivated is to treat them the way *they* want to be treated, and not the way *you* want to be treated," she states. "I heard this from my first boss at Philips, and I've used this tip to build different interaction styles to deal with different people in the business world."

"As a supply chain manager, you need to think of ways to bring people together to collaborate and provide them with the right data to make meaningful decisions. I've experienced this shift strongly since the advent of the pandemic, both on the customer and the supplier side. A lot of heated emotions are involved when a crisis strikes. That's when facts and data help you perform a root cause analysis. You can use this analysis to work toward risk mitigation

191

plans should such a situation arise in the future."

Praeceptor contends that the relationships Mondi invested in before the pandemic helped during its difficult times, especially when things were out of the organization's control — such as when rising energy costs led the company's operational costs to skyrocket. "But even when there were risks involved, our customers trusted and relied on us to produce and deliver. Investing in relationships paid us back with value additions," she says.

Another facet to being a people leader is to realize that not everything goes according to plan. "The complexity of supply chain management makes it impossible to get everything right. It helps to have the Sprint Mentality, where you are fully engaged and then fully disengaged once the situation crosses over. If the outcome of a Sprint is good enough to proceed, you should push it and do the rest of the things on the go," Praeceptor says.

"To me, the idea of a quintessential people leader has nothing to do with the supply chain. It's about how you're never good enough to [not] be kind to people. This has stuck with me right from the start of my career. In the end, we are only as good as the people we work with, and the sooner we internalize kindness, the better we will be with our people, and the better they will be with our organization."

Scan the QR code below or visit www.sourcetosold.com to access exclusive bonus content you can use with your teams to further explore the concepts and insights covered in this book.

CHAPTER 20:

CHOUAIB ROKBI

"Trust your guts and brains. I've noticed some people lose their common sense and even their conscience at their workplace, often [doing] things they would never do at home."

Chouaib Rokbi is executive vice president of digital transformation and information technology at the European semiconductor manufacturer STMicroelectronics. Joining ST in 2000 as industrial controller for its plant in Rousset, France, he proceeded to hold a series of senior positions in financial control, efficiency improvement programs, and corporate strategic initiatives. In 2018, Rokbi was appointed chief transformation officer and tasked with rebuilding the company's main operational processes, including supply chain, product life-cycle management, and manufacturing analytics.

Amongst leaders that spend most of their waking hours contemplating challenges in the supply chain, Chouaib Rokbi cuts a different image. "My experiences have led me to have an unconventional approach to work," he says. "While being focused at work is essential, I advise people to not adopt a perspective that makes them approach work like their life depends on it. Supply chain is a place where you strive to make the world a better place, but not at the risk of a personal burn out."

This approach dates back to an experience Rokbi had during his earlier career as a mechanical engineer designing and building machines for hard rock mining. As part of his duties, Rokbi had to visit client mining locations worldwide to deploy machines and gather feedback on their functioning. "These endeavors took me to countries in Africa, to places that weren't usually visitor friendly or safe," he recalls. "On one occasion, I travelled to Zambia to visit one of their National Copper Company's mining locations."

Upon reaching the location, Rokbi spoke to the mine director, who gave him instructions on how to travel down the mine to check the machinery. This was an arduous expedition in itself, requiring approximately two hours to reach the machine from the surface. "We had to first reach down to the mine through a shaft, walk for two kilometers to reach the next shaft, reach down from there and walk a couple more kilometers to finally reach the location where the machine was located to see the machine in action and carry out our inspection," says Rokbi.

And so Rokbi went, accompanied by a colleague from Tamrock and a Zambian technician from the mine. At the location, Rokbi saw people using the drill-and-blast method of mining, in which dynamite is detonated beneath the soil and the gravel then taken out to recover the ore. As this is an extremely risky process, mines need support pillars around them to stop them from caving in and burying people inside.

"After spending a while at the bottom of the mine, I somehow felt it was time to leave," recounts Rokbi. "The two [other] guys insisted on staying, but as I refused, all three of us left the cave. Two hours later, I heard that the bottom of the mine had collapsed and four people had died.

"It's been twenty-three years since that fateful day, and I still don't know what struck me to leave at that moment."

This episode has stuck with Rokbi throughout his career, and given him two lessons to live by. "My first learning is not to risk your life for your job. The second takeaway is to trust your guts and brains. I've noticed in my career that people leave their gut feelings and even their conscience behind when they come to work. This needs to change."

As head of supply chain transformation and IT at ST Microelectronics, Rokbi encourages the people around him to actively question processes and the way the supply chain is executed today to make sure to aim for continuous improvement and change. "Keep a fresh eye. You must always have an open eye on what is happening around you to enable a proper reaction. Especially in these disruptive times, you should always ask whether things make sense around you and whether you and your organization are agile enough to respond."

THE NEED FOR QUESTIONING
LEADERSHIP IN THE WORKPLACE

For Rokbi, a light-hearted sense of humor comes in handy to make the workplace more relaxed and conducive to disagreement, whether you're designing a new demand planning process, setting up the future supply chain organization, or determining how to best run an S&OP meeting. "I like it when my people disagree with me; it makes me feel like I'm being challenged intellectually," he says. "The more they disagree, the more we build and learn together. When I'm throwing ideas at people, I want them to consider them as ideas, and not as hard-and-fast truths. I want people around me to challenge me, and I invite my team to do the same — jointly, we always reach the best solution for the company."

Rokbi argues that the culture of speaking up and challenging the boss in a healthy manner should be more encouraged within organizations. "Debate will truly lead to better solutions. Rewarding a culture of questioning and disagreement is critical, as it demands that leaders question the status quo and remain conducive to change."

"When you realize and admit you made a mistake, you can change things for the better. Flexibility in your ideas is key."

"Every organization is made of two kinds of managers," contends Rokbi. The first kind are those who do not take kindly to losing face, which, according to him, creates an environment where employees cannot confront managers on their decisions, and thus fosters a culture of obedience.

Rokbi considers himself the second type of manager: those who defend their opinions with solid logic, but are ready to listen if someone has a great idea. "If you exhibit the latter kind of leadership, you can lead by example and change the way people think," he asserts. "As a leader, you should be proud but know when to step back and admit your ideas don't fly. You might have strong opinions, but you should be okay with rethinking them and understand that it's not the end of the world for you. When you realize and admit you made a mistake, you can change things for the better. Flexibility in your ideas is key."

This behavior is crucial in the complex transformational environment Rokbi was leading: working on updated processes, ways of working, organizational structure, and an integrated IT backbone puts ongoing challenges to the leaders. To add even more complexity on top, the pandemic hit, which made preparing for the future and drawing up a forecast extremely challenging. In an extreme situation such as this, if a leader is not flexible the company can set itself up for failure. This is why, for Rokbi, it is crucial that a leader not fall in love with a single idea, but rather stay flexible if the environment does change.

"Dissociate your work ideas from your identity — this will allow you to go back and question them," he says. "There's no need to put your self-esteem alongside your decisions at work. When facts in the business world change, work opinions change too. Assuming you're correct 90% of the time, it is sensible to leave 10% room to shift. Being agile and adapting to the changing environment is what makes a great leader."

TRANSFORMING AN ORGANIZATION BY CREATING ENGAGEMENT

Supply chain transformation is complex, as it covers the end-to-end value chain from a strategic to an operational level. In addition, Rokbi says that a lot of the context gets lost in translation across the organization. Industry jargon can perplex people who hail from, say, an engineering background.

"At ST, the first four supply chain transformations were not successful. It was only the fifth one that came through. When I looked back on the reasons, I realized we were trying to fix the consequences instead of looking at the problem holistically. While we suggested improvements to speed up the [IT] systems, we refused to dig into the issues' roots. Only when we started to work on the root causes were we able to improve the performance of the overall supply chain significantly and lastingly."

One of the issues Rokbi regularly contends with is people who can't express precisely what they want or say things they don't mean, which is challenging in a complex supply chain transformation. "In this context, I tell my people to read personalities laterally. I always ask my people to wait before they start thinking of solutions to people's problems and try to understand where their problems come from, what the root causes and, therefore, the solutions are."

Sustaining momentum can often be problematic when organizations pursue transformation, as it can start to dwindle after reaching a crest. Rokbi explains that his company held its transformation attempts together by formalizing a vision before working out the details. This involved redefining how the company looked at the value chain, and changing perspectives on the basic framework for transformation.

"When you embed transformation into the day-to-day lives of your people, it's easier for them to grasp its essence. You need to make them understand what the company is doing and why they are doing it," says Rokbi. "We've placed the supply chain and the product R&D at the center of our value chain, which has helped us put things into perspective whenever anything gets off track."

Putting the focus on only a single metric like EBITDA or cost reduction is not enough. Rokbi points out how his team creates various scenarios balancing gross margins and R&D, as this lays the ground for the future and toward sustainable growth. "Customers come to us because we design and serve products to the specifications they ask for, not because we have a great backbone or because we're able to deliver in a day. It's critical to ensure every cog in the wheel is aligned to the common framework when you're in business — be it finance, sales, operations, R&D, or even fund management."

For a chief transformation officer, bringing change entails understanding the processes that can be improved within the organization, and for the people at the top to clearly communicate the need for change with a sense of urgency. In Rokbi's experience this is often not the case, as the top management can be slow to change.

"Unless the leaders change, the chief transformation officer can't move the facilities at the center of bringing a transformation in an organization," he says. "Transforming is about moving things, which is impossible if you don't have strong engagement from the people at the top. Having a vested interest in the change is a start, but people at the top need to possess energy, share a belief in change, and get themselves involved."

BUILDING A SUPPLY CHAIN THAT CREATES AND CAPTURES VALUE

"At the end of the day, the supply chain is a process that lets you take an order from a customer and deliver it to them on time and at the right quality," declares Rokbi. "This means understanding what the customer wants, serving them the right product, and shipping it where needed. It could get complex depending on various macro-economic factors, but the process remains the same by and large."

Within organizations, this fundamental process will run up against the true resiliency of their supply chains. In the automotive supply chain, for example, major OEMs are increasingly dependent on raw materials and parts sourced from regions with questionable supply consistency, such as areas with autocratic regimes or regions that are in conflict. "We've witnessed industries struggle to adapt to changing times. The disruption of the value chains caused by the pandemic was so drastic that we now live in a world where we've shifted from value capturing to value creation," says Rokbi. "Companies that don't plan their roadmap properly often have the challenge of a messy supply chain. This can only be solved by proper end-to-end planning and execution and an agile and forward-looking organization."

Rokbi points out that companies in the West are especially impacted by their decisions to leave manufacturing to Asia Pacific, which has made them vulnerable to disruption. "The semiconductor crisis triggered at the advent of the pandemic shed some light on how global supply chains could stall due to issues in a specific region that has monopolized production," he says. "I've been discussing this important topic for 20 years now — companies weren't interested in manufacturing for a long time and depended on third parties.

"Today, the question supply chain stakeholders have to answer is not who earns money, but who that money ends up with. As is the case in the semiconductor industry, companies that can't reconsolidate their supply chains will find that while they could be making money right now, the value will ultimately go to the company that is irreplaceable in the value chain."

A 360-degree understanding of supply chains will help, contends Rokbi. "Transforming a company means understanding technology, finance, and strategy. I went about this by getting an engineering degree followed by an MBA, which set me on a path to getting a complete view of the business and financial world. The transformation I'm part of allows me to act as an all-rounder in the company, the segment's biggest selling point.

"There's always something fun and exciting to be done here, and if you're like me, this vantage point is the best place to work in the industry."

Scan the QR code below or visit www.sourcetosold.com to access exclusive bonus content you can use with your teams to further explore the concepts and insights covered in this book.

CHAPTER 21:

JIM ROWAN

"It is really important that senior leadership
embrace a mindset of lifelong learning."

Jim Rowan is the president and CEO of Volvo Cars, a position he has held since March 2022. He previously spent eight years at Dyson, joining the organization as a board member and COO in 2012 before being appointed CEO five years later. He has also held senior positions at a variety of other major organizations, including BlackBerry (COO, 2007–2012), Celestica (EVP of global operations, 2005–2007) and Flex (VP of European operations, 1998–2005).

Although he's transitioned to the post of chief executive, Jim Rowan still places great importance on maintaining a comprehensive understanding of end-to-end supply chains. "I find it imperative to understand all tiers of the supply chain. For building a sustainable company and a well-governed organization compliant with the latest government regulations, it's critical to understand its supply chain," he says.

"I take time to understand the fundamentals. For instance, I try to have an overview of demand and supply planning across not just the Tier 1 supplier base, but also the levels below that. While this is a lot of work, it helps me figure out where the fracture points are; it's a perception that comes in handy when there's a disruption."

Unlike some of his peers, Rowan took a more traditional route to the supply chain, after starting out as a manufacturing apprentice. "I learned at a young age how to deal with shop-floor dynamics," he recalls. "I realized manufacturing was one of the biggest contributors to a reliable and efficient production ecosystem. A lot of the challenges in the supply chain can be traced back to issues with raw material/components delivery or quality. I saw firsthand that the easiest way to ensure an efficient supply chain is to have a reliable supply of subassemblies, raw materials and components."

Rowan has learned invaluable lessons from the supply chain over the course of his three-decade career. "I'm good at assessing competitors in the market and in cherry-picking strategies that will do well within the supply chain," he says. "I honed this trait while at Flex, heading a dozen of their factories spread across Europe. We worked with customers renowned in the electronics space, which gave me a bird's-eye view of their supply chains and allowed me to analyze strategies and optimize logistics operations objectively. These are skills that I bank on as a leader even today. Everyone talks about data analytics now, but in the supply chain, it's always been about the data."

EMOTIONAL INTELLIGENCE AS THE CORNERSTONE OF INSPIRED LEADERSHIP

Rowan believes that emotional intelligence is an essential catalyst for effecting positive change on operations. "Although I was on the operational side of the business, my work wasn't only analytical. I dealt with numbers on spreadsheets, but building relationships with people was an important part of the job," he says.

"Emotional intelligence is something that some people have naturally, but it is a skill that can be learned. Early on in my career my work took me across different countries, ones where I didn't speak the local language. But to be a leader I had to try and quickly understand their culture, as it is essential to building a strong team."

One of those destinations was Vienna, where Rowan lived for four years heading Eastern European operations for Flex, with factories in Hungary, the Czech Republic, Poland, and Ukraine. At this time Eastern Europe was a burgeoning manufacturing hub, and people from all over were migrating to industrialized cities in search of work. "There was a lot of variety in the workforce, with people coming from all over Europe and beyond. It was a great learning experience working with all of them and communicating beyond the apparent language barriers. Working in a cultural melting pot really helped me understand what makes people from different places tick," Rowan says.

"Ultimately, the supply chain is a people's business, no matter what you're building. It's about getting the best from individuals and building strong, cross-functional teams. This comes with experience — I don't think you can learn how to truly engage with people [by reading] a book. You have to lend an ear to individuals, to their perspectives, and [then] you realize there's always something to learn."

Rowan cites Mike McNamara, the CEO of Flex during his tenure there, as an example of the leadership style he's describing. "He was a fantastic mentor who pushed you hard, but let you make your own decisions. He maintained that you could learn more from wrong decisions than from successful ones. While he kept an eye on big-ticket items, he let you control decisions that had a significant impact on operations — and in the case of you making a mistake, he allowed you to recover from the situation and learn from it. I think this approach to leadership is crucial to building individuals that carry the company forward, helping build strong succession in the planning process."

LEADERSHIP NEEDS TO STAY CONSTANTLY RELEVANT

While many chief executives are reluctant to embrace social media, Rowan touts the benefits of top management engaging with platforms like Instagram, Facebook, and Snapchat. "I believe there's tremendous reasoning behind searching for ways to remain relevant [by] unlearning and relearning social interaction, especially in a world that's becoming increasingly digital," he opines.

"When I was at Dyson, I took mentorship under people who I call digital natives. These are young people who've grown up in the digital world. I started my career in the analog generation, and as a result my brain was hardwired to think from an analog perspective.

"These digital natives relate to the digital world quite differently. To ensure seamless interaction, I tried to learn how to rewire my brain to think digital-first. That's just one example of how to remain fresh and relevant as technology and cultures change. It is really important that senior leadership embrace a mindset of lifelong learning."

According to Rowan, understanding the digital world directly influenced him to build strategies to grow B2C sales. "I observe digital natives to understand how they interact on social media. What are the norms? What's the length of the sentences? How do they construct them? Who do they interact with on these platforms? Understanding these social media nuances across various platforms helps me define B2C sales strategies while thinking of ways to get the message across to my customers, such as engaging influencers, key opinion leaders, and choosing the right social media channels."

With two teenagers at home during the pandemic, Rowan received even more education about how the digital-native generation both navigates and drives this new environment. "My 16-year-old got his first bank account during the pandemic but has never had a credit card and never feels the need to have cash, as all his transactions are digital," notes Rowan. "While teenagers don't directly drive sales, they already greatly influence it. They are educating their parents and the older generation with brand insights that would have hardly mattered before — like information on how mindful companies are about sustainability. Give Gen Z a few more years till they have a wallet of their own, and we will see a seismic change in the way companies position themselves in the market."

In the here and now, meanwhile, Rowan emphasizes that companies and their management must stay current with the technological times. "Today, you have to be comfortable with multiple video-conferencing platforms, be it Zoom, Teams, or FaceTime. Most people are working from home, and often across multiple time zones. You can't rely on having an assistant to connect you to your video conference — you have to be really comfortable doing all this yourself.

"In the same way, if you are looking to create traction in the digital world, you must learn to consume it first," he continues. "Staying relevant today means being digitally fluent. In fact, I'd go out on a limb and say that digital quotient (DQ) is as important today as IQ and EQ."

THE IMPORTANCE OF SUPPLY CHAIN TO ORGANIZATIONAL FUNCTIONING

Rowan contends that the supply chain continues to be an underrated vertical within many companies. "There are several points of entry and exit within the supply chain, [which makes it] complex to comprehend. If you go to a Tier 3 supply chain, there's so much diversity in geographies, company sizes, physical locations, networks, and software. Smaller companies downstream even lack proper systems like an ERP or MES, as many still use Excel to run their business.

"I think it's unfathomable for a lot of people to get a complete end-to-end understanding of the supply chain. But again, why should they feel the need to understand that? We, the people in the supply chain, are on the watchtower looking out for them, and that's our job."

Today, however, senior leadership across organizations globally are awakening to that complexity, as well as the supply chain management prowess required to steward a company through multiple black swan events, be it global financial crises, environmental or public health disasters, political disruptions, armed conflicts, and more. Rowan acknowledges that he's been lucky to have enjoyed decent top-level engagement with the supply chain in his career, which is not the case in many other organizations. "Many companies continue to look at supply chains as a service and outsource them, missing out on optimizing a crucial segment that contributes to their bottom line," he says.

"It ultimately boils down to understanding the company fundamentals. As the CEO of operational businesses, I've understood them at the most visceral level. I have a fair idea of important building blocks that make up a successful organization, such as what makes the company tick, what makes them money, and what makes them lose it."

Transitioning from COO to CEO helped Rowan understand the technology the company pioneered and the supply chain that helped deliver the products to their customers. "I connected with sales guys all the way to the ground level. They were my connection to the real world, where I got vital information to improve my SOP process. I tried putting myself in the shoes of my ground staff to build insights that I could channel into my business.

"The single biggest piece of advice I can give is to listen and connect with people to understand what's important for the business."

BUILDING A ROBUST SUPPLY CHAIN IN A DISRUPTIVE ENVIRONMENT

Rowan laments that supply chain operations remain an unglamorous field for many in business, even as it continues to be of such critical importance in maintaining the health of an organization. "It's easy to think of the supply chain as invisible when it works well. It's like the air that you breathe. You take air for granted until the minute something goes wrong, and you start gasping for breath. While you're able to sense that immediately, it most probably is a major problem already.

"Take the case of just-in-time (JIT) manufacturing. While JIT can help companies maintain a lean supply chain and preserve cash, it does little to build robustness into supply planning. True robustness would help sense early warning signs of when things start to break down. The cardinal duty of the supply chain is to ensure we move products through the pipeline, irrespective of congested ports, lack of freight capacity, inclement weather conditions, or a drawn-out pandemic. Uninterrupted operations are the hallmark of an efficient and resilient supply chain.

> "It's easy to think of the supply chain as invisible when it works well. It's like the air that you breathe. You take air for granted until the minute something goes wrong, and you start gasping for breath."

"Companies need to develop more tolerance of inventory and, in some cases, reduce their distance to market. They need to create more resilience and flexibility, especially as more and more products are being bought online with no forecast or previous demand data to reference."

This is all the more important as the hemispheric balance shifts. In the past, production was concentrated in the East and consumption in the West; however, that is now quickly changing, due to many reasons. For instance, the increase in duty tariffs between the US and China adversely impacted businesses, and will continue to create stress in operations — particularly for companies that do not factor these changes into their future business models and simply seek to operate as they did before.

Rowan highlights how the increasingly erratic nature of consumer trends today stands in stark contrast to the last few decades, when companies could reasonably predict demand based on sales history. "You could determine future sales based on internal catalogues, promotions, and the onset of events such as Christmas or Black Friday. But with the emergence of digital channels, it's much harder to anticipate demand."

For this reason, Rowan recommends holding products at their late-stage configuration, keeping the demand for expedited fulfillment in mind. "You need to have the core product ready. Additions such as color and shade can be added before putting it in the box. Companies that adopt such approaches will likely be more successful when they transition to digital channels," he contends.

"This approach works well today because people want mass personalization. Apple can stick to building a few models because personalization on its iPhone is via an application layer that enables users to design their home screen. Ultimately, this makes an iPhone feel like a personal product you want to carry around in your pocket. This is one way manufacturers can meet the demand for personalization without personalizing the product during the build stage."

In Rowan's view, companies that have built more resilience in their supply chains will learn to adapt better to adversity, inevitably out-lasting market competitors that only look at logistics operations as a cost center. "People will rely on multiple alternate part suppliers and plan for extra inventory wherever possible to be more tolerable, operate flexibly, and deal with breakdowns," he predicts. "Regional manufacturing is going to experience a boost. The world will see a huge shift in the global manufacturing patterns.

"We can already see that goods once manufactured in China for global distribution are now manufactured in China, for China. Regional manufacturing, or at least regional late-stage configuration, is becoming much more of a trend."

Asked to offer some parting advice about how management should navigate the evolving supply chain landscape, Rowan declares that "You need to consider what will work best for your company, your products and, ultimately, your customers. There is no 'one size fits all' — take the time to analyze the data and design a supply chain that is not only robust and resilient, but will also provide some level of flexibility in the face of disruption. And at the same time, make the effort and build the trust to develop long-term relationships with your key suppliers."

Scan the QR code below or visit www.sourcetosold.com to access exclusive bonus content you can use with your teams to further explore the concepts and insights covered in this book.

CHAPTER 22:

YOSSI SHEFFI

"As a CEO, you must project optimism. This means keeping yourself in a good mood and, most importantly, raising the spirits of your team and keeping morale up after a disappointment."

Yossi Sheffi is the director of the MIT Center for Transportation & Logistics (MIT CTL) and director and founder of the institution's Master of Engineering in Logistics program. Under his leadership the MIT CTL has launched many educational, research, and industry/government outreach programs, and he also spearheaded an international expansion of the Center to Spain, Latin America, China, Malaysia and Luxembourg. Outside of academia he has founded or co-founded five successful logistics companies and authored six books, the latest of which, *A Shot in the Arm: How Science, Engineering, and Supply Chains Converged to Vaccinate the World*, was published in October 2021.

Over several decades of teaching at the Massachusetts Institute of Technology (MIT), Yossi Sheffi has routinely been asked by students how he seems to have remained unfazed when things went wrong for him in the business world — especially while he was steering one of the companies he founded and subsequently sold through the depths of the dot-com crash. For Sheffi — who served in the Israeli Air Force for five years and has travelled the world extensively, including visits to many developing countries — the reason is simple. "When you live in a free society where there is little danger of hunger or violence, struggles and even failures in business are just experiences and never a calamity," he observes.

Sheffi's illustrious career has seen him serve as the director of the MIT Center for Transportation and Logistics since 1992, author hundreds of scientific papers and six award-winning books, and found or co-found five companies — one of which, the third-party logistics start-up Logi-Corp, reached $600 million in revenues before it was acquired by Ryder System in 1994. Explaining why he has continued to shuttle between lecture halls and board meetings, Sheffi says that "I have been able to translate the latest research available in the industry into technology solutions, and, at the same time, bring industry examples to my students through case studies from my own experience."

Only a few years into his academic career, Sheffi began looking for ways to apply his work in the real world. "After several years of studying and researching urban transportation planning, I wrote my first book, *Urban Transportation Networks: Equilibrium Analysis with Mathematical Programming Methods*. But at this point in my career, I already realized that implementing innovations in the public sector was not happening easily. My best ideas ended up in scientific papers and books, but I wanted to see them implemented.

"So I ended up using the network theory and algorithms developed as part of my urban network research to optimize trucking networks. This work became the foundation for my first start-up, Princeton Transportation Consulting Group (PTCG), which I founded with three colleagues in 1987," and which went on to develop software-based decision support systems for the trucking industry and, later, for manufacturers and retailers as well. After a turbulent initial period, Sheffi took over as chief executive of the company in 1993. Three years later, he sold PTCG to Sabre Holdings, a part of AMR, which is owned by American Airlines.

It was here that Sheffi had a first, painful lesson in the realities of mergers and acquisitions. Sabre took PTCG, a relatively small entrepreneurial firm, and tried fitting it into its idea of a bigger, more established corporation. Employees who had no titles before were immediately divided into five ranks. The size of each cubicle had to reflect the rank of the employee, as did the allocation of parking spaces and the ability to get free flights on American Airlines. This imposing of classifications, ranks and benefits had disastrous consequences. It demoralized employees, fractured the company's collaborative culture, and resulted in PTCG transforming from a profit-accruing to a loss-making entity.

Incensed with what had happened with the company, Sheffi bought PTCG back, intending to turn its fortunes around. "I knew the people and knew what went into the various software algorithms behind our solutions. And I knew the people were solid and that they believed in me," he recalls. "I had a good VC backup, and I quickly bought another local company and merged the two. That helped the culture because the other company was also a start-up, giving us an infusion of several great people."

Sheffi asserts that acquisitions work well when the acquired company keeps its culture intact rather than being pushed quickly toward complete integration within the parent company. This is particularly true when the acquiring company is traditional and the acquired is small and entrepreneurial. Such integrations take a long time if they are to be done well, as they are tricky to execute.

When it came time to sell his next company, LogiCorp, to Ryder, Sheffi and his partner insisted on setting the terms by which the firm would be incorporated into the transportation giant. "The going-in position was, 'Don't Ryderize this company.' And they left it alone for a long time. Now, what used to be LogiCorp is a multibillion dollar part of Ryder," says Sheffi with satisfaction.

BEING AN IMPACT CEO

In Sheffi's view, the fundamental prerequisite to being a CEO is understanding the business and what makes it work. Chief supply chain officers are naturals for the role of a CEO, because they under-stand the entire operation. That said, Sheffi cautions against CSCOs banking solely on their supply chain experience. "Successful moves into the CEO position require understanding the other parts of the business [as well], from innovation and R&D to marketing and sales," he advises.

The most important characteristic of any leader at any level, however, is the ability to hire great people and motivate them to do their best. "There's nothing more important than hiring and developing people — ones that are even better than yourself," Sheffi says. "Leaders understand that their success is based on the success of the team around them."

Furthermore, leaders understand that the difference between good and excellent people is very large. "For example, the gap between the performance of an excellent software engineer and a good one is not times-two — it is times-ten, and it takes some time for companies to recognize this. I have sat on the advisory boards of several companies, and I see managers and even CEOs in trouble all the time [because of this]. They hire too fast, without due diligence, and end up losing time and resources while doing it."

> "There's nothing more important than hiring and developing people — ones that are even better than yourself. Leaders understand that their success is based on the success of the team around them."

While being a leader can be relatively easy going when conditions are favorable, the true test of a CEO's fortitude is when the going gets tough — a crucible that Sheffi had to endure during the dot-com crash. "When the tech bubble burst, I had to let go of almost half the people I hired. And those people have families. This got to me, and I could not sleep well for several weeks. But when the morale is low, it is up to the CEO to show confidence and push through." This is especially true for small companies, in which peaks and valleys are the norm. "As a CEO, you must project optimism. This means keeping yourself in a good mood and, most importantly, raising the spirits of your team and keeping morale up after a disappointment," Sheffi observes.

Conversely, of course, it's equally essential to morale to celebrate successes, which Sheffi did with his team every time they landed a big client. He recalls how, in one of his companies, employees displayed scientific papers on the walls whose authors "[could not] solve the type of mathematical optimization problems that the company was solving routinely. We wanted to build the pride of the organization in what we were doing. We also encouraged people to get involved in the universities nearby, giving lectures and also writing scientific papers. The idea was not to be a gladiator of mathematical solutions, but to make a big deal out of scientific successes, which helps keep the team motivated."

Speaking to the question of raising capital for start-ups, Sheffi observes that "There's always a problem of when to take money and how much to take. The general rule of thumb is to take it before you absolutely need it. You shouldn't be pushed to a corner where you're negotiating with a VC when the business is about to go under.

"One of the mistakes I made with one of the companies was taking too much money too early. The problem was not giving up equity: the main problem is that people developed bad habits and were not watching the pennies. They start acting as if they are employed by a big and rich company, rather than being committed to success."

Sheffi observes that it is typical for companies to act too late once things go bad. "I have made that mistake too. In the case of things going wrong, and the company starts burning cash with no end in sight, act decisively. Waiting for the situation to improve on its own rarely works.

"And if you're an entrepreneur building a business, don't even think of having a work-life balance," Sheffi adds. "If you're launching a start-up, you will work harder than you ever did, so you better do something you are very passionate about. If you have a family, make sure they are on board for several tough years."

BEING A SUPPLY CHAIN TORCHBEARER

"In my opinion, supply chain thinking should be everywhere," Sheffi declares. "Every process, invention, or service contains a series of processes and activities. In that sense, supply chain thinking is fundamental to the delivery of any product, service, innovation, university lecture, whatever.

"Naturally, though, some supply chains are significantly more complex than others," he adds. As an example, he points to automotive supply chains, which are a combination of multiple supply chains that are spun off for the different products and components needed to build a vehicle. The auto industry comprises technology supply chains alongside supply chains for commodities like metal, plastic, and thousands of parts, each of which spins off a complex supply chain of its own. "The supply chains of contract manufacturers like Flex or Jabil are even more complex, due to the variety of products they build and industries they serve," Sheffi observes.

"What I find fascinating is that supply chains combine multiple elements — processes, technologies, relationships, innovations — all managed by people all over the globe with different backgrounds, cultures, and subject to various legal and societal regimes. And it all works like an orchestra without a single conductor. In some sense, the reason that it all works — what GM used to call 'the daily miracle' — is a testament to the human spirit and ingenuity."

Given that high-flown endorsement, Sheffi is gratified to note that interest in joining the supply chain community has been on the rise following a long period of decline — due not only to the unglamorous associations that the supply chain had for so many, but a dearth of training programs that could prepare people for a career in the field. Sheffi attests that MIT recognized this problem in the late 1990s, when its Center for Transportation & Logistics could only graduate forty students a year from its master's program.

In response, says Sheffi, "we decided to open centers around the world to graduate more students." This initiative resulted in the establishment of satellite campuses in Colombia, Spain, Luxembourg, Malaysia, and China, which helped MIT propel many more graduates into the field. Even this, however, was not enough to fulfill the worldwide need for more supply chain talent, which led the center to launch an online MicroMaster program of five online courses with comprehensive exams.

"The program attracted over 480,000 learners, surpassing all expectations," Sheffi recalls. "The students receive a certificate, and the top one can attend MIT and get a full master's degree in a single semester. Twenty-one other universities have recognized the Micro-Master certificate in supply chain management from MIT, and allow students to graduate in a short time. Online courses from institutions like MIT serve as a gateway for elite education, reaching a large number of people who could not enroll physically on campus.

The demand for online supply chain courses represents a sea change in the industry, opening avenues for bright minds to move up the ladder. And, with more people from more diverse backgrounds now engaged in supply chains, and the increasing emphasis on supply chain operations, there are more opportunities for CSCOs to move to the helm of the companies they work in.

THE QUALITIES THAT MAKE A CEO

"There is no secret sauce to becoming a CEO," Sheffi says. "A

CSCO should be obviously successful at the position. The CSCO should make sure that they get the attention of the board. The board should know you, and you must make sure you have a good interaction with the members. While you may or may not be the next CEO of your own company, board members serve on other boards and can open other opportunities.

"Speaking their language is key," he continues. "A good CSCO will tie supply chain metrics to the financial and Wall Street metrics that the board is concerned about. Linking inventory turns and procurement policies to stock prices will show the board the impact of supply chain practices on the corporation."

Sheffi also notes the need for lifelong learning at every position, calling it a "survival mechanism" in an environment where there is a constant need to keep improving skills and expertise for fear of becoming irrelevant. "Last year, I took time to learn Python because my students were using it, and I did not understand what they were doing. And that was frightening. Reinventing yourself is critical, whether you're in technology, marketing, or business," he asserts. In the supply chain world, part of learning is to connect with industry thought leaders, attend conferences, and listen to people, as well as taking advantage of the voluminous amount of material that is available online (which, Sheffi contends, makes gaining knowledge far easier today than it was a decade ago).

The reason why such learning is particularly crucial for supply chain professionals, Sheffi insists, is that "supply chain adds fundamental value. It affects both revenue and cost, while many other functions are supporting actors to the provision of real value. Good supply chain practitioners have to understand feedback loops, non-linear behavior, risk and uncertainty, as well as advanced technology."

At the same time, Sheffi adds, "supply chain management involves people and relationships. Thus, understanding global attitudes and practices is important — and fascinating. Gaining this perspective helps a supply chain officer to become more of a 'people person,' which will ultimately help them in every facet of their career — be it with their current jobs, or while searching for their next one."

Scan the QR code below or visit www.sourcetosold.com to access exclusive bonus content you can use with your teams to further explore the concepts and insights covered in this book.

CHAPTER 23:

PIER LUIGI SIGISMONDI

"You can make your job meaningful no matter what you do in life, how many people you lead, or which products you handle. It does not need to sound sexy to be meaningful and impactful for the world."

Pier Luigi Sigismondi is the president of Dole Sunshine Company, where he is currently leading a transformation to remake the legacy brand into a leading nutrition and wellness company. Prior to joining Dole in 2019 he spent nine years at Unilever — joining in 2009 as chief supply chain officer and rising to the position of president for Southeast Asia and Australasia — and seven years at Nestlé, as VP of corporate operations strategies in Switzerland and then as VP of operations and R&D for Nestlé Mexico.

With a career that spans thirty years and, as the president of Dole, now heading one of the largest FMCG companies in the world, Pier Luigi Sigismondi has seen and built organizations that stand the test of time. Early in his career, however, "it was a lot of work to transition from an academic background to the business world," he recalls. "Along with my strong analytical skills, I applied all my energy to understanding and seeking ways to deliver in the real world. It was clear that success was not just about learning, but the execution of tangible and long-lasting change on the shop floor. That was probably my first lesson venturing into the business environment.

"I have a master's in industrial engineering from Georgia Institute of Technology, a premier engineering school. But to work in the industry, I had to completely evolve from being an intense academic to an operations professional. I worked night shifts in factories and interacted with my fellow workers. The blue-collar experience put humility in me, and showed me the importance of the labor that drives companies at their fundamental level."

Sigismondi contends that for a company to truly leverage supply chain operations, it is critical to listen to consumer feedback and channel it upstream to improve products and services. "During my role as country head of the supply chain at Nestlé, we learned how to deploy market research, sales analytics, and consumer insights to improve product development and route-to-market efforts. While people in the supply chain have traditionally had friction working with the marketing and sales teams, I made it a point to work closely with them to design experimental centers to better understand consumer behavior."

One of Sigismondi's most ambitious initiatives in this vein was inspired by his memories in Venezuela as a little boy, where he remembers a visit to a juice factory and being amazed by the fresh taste and cards the company gave out that smelled like their flavors. Decades later at Nestlé, he spearheaded a plan that transformed the company's confectionary factory into "an amazing chocolate kingdom for kids. Tens of thousands of kids visited a magic place with brand characters and all operators dressed like *Charlie and the Chocolate Factory* characters. We created tunnels, painted the walls, and immersed the students into a brand and product experience like never before. This helped us link marketing insights to supply chain operations, enabling us to build consumers engaged with our brands for life like no other company had ever done before."

Reflecting on that fateful childhood trip to Caracas, Sigismondi maintains that "Those memories helped me create fantastic customer experiences many years down the line, because I clearly understood that these instances stay with you forever. My personal purpose is building a legacy that can last for generations. Using my experience to build brands, people, factories, and distribution networks to make a difference to the business excites me."

GOOD LEADERSHIP NEEDS A GRASP OF END-TO-END BUSINESS

"To achieve impact in the supply chain, it's important to understand what it means to operate a business. Think of the end-to-end supply chain as the backbone for a human that keeps everything together — it keeps the vital organs in place, and strengthens the joints to walk and grab things," Sigismondi says.

"A leader of an end-to-end supply chain must understand operations right from the moment specifications are defined to when the product sits on the shelf. This will help build the right planning processes to ensure that replenishments flow seamlessly."

A comprehensive understanding of operations is key to building resilience. For example, the pandemic has pushed companies to transition from "just-in-time" to "just-in-case," building an inventory buffer to circumvent future large-scale disruptions. Sigismondi contends that while predicting the future is by no means easy, it is still worthwhile and practical to posit what-if scenarios and have potential responses worked out to prevent supply chain shock.

"Organizations need to classify resources into two categories of people — those who design, and those who deliver. These are profoundly different types of individuals: one develops systems, competencies, and long-term strategy for the company, and the other [translates] those skills and strategies into sustained change. As a leader, you have to consciously ensure you have people allocated on both fronts in the best possible way. Otherwise, you're going to always [need to] catch up or [you'll] have your plans stuck on

PowerPoint. Just thinking about the future does not deliver value."

Sigismondi says that several factors can set a company up for growth. "You need to differentiate yourself in the market, which comes with being responsive to consumer feedback, speed-to-market innovation, and building lasting consumer experiences. These factors help the business grow and yield higher margins and revenue. An end-to-end supply chain isn't just about good functionality, it's also about building outstanding operations that are tuned for growth. Ultimately, it all boils down to how you can add more value."

Good leadership is also about recruiting the right people. "I value people not just for the depth of knowledge they have, but also for the breadth of their decision-making skills. That's my advice to anyone — to keep stretching all the time. Ask yourself what decision you'd have taken if you were in that person's shoes.

"At Dole, against common wisdom, I brought into the team a passionate, failed start-up founder. She works tirelessly with her team members to bring innovation and inspiration from the outside world to Dole. She helped us replace chemical sterilization of raw materials with electrical processes that kill the bacteria without treating them with fertilizers or pesticides — a significant step up in protecting the product's safety without harming the environment."

MANAGING DEMAND AND SUPPLY IN THE TIME OF COVID

While the term "unprecedented" has been used frequently in describing the pandemic's impact on global businesses, Sigismondi says that he has truly never seen the likes of what Dole experienced during the COVID era.

"At the height of the pandemic we had to respond to the historically high demand, but with significant labor constraints. People in the factories were afraid of getting infected, and we had to tighten safety provisions in our operations," he says. "This was a catch-22 situation: while we had the opportunity to shape and deliver to the demand, we could not source enough supply. It was an unpredictable reality with [all the] constraints, [but] we optimized our resources to the maximum extent. While we did lose sales, we still ended up growing 13 percent in 2021, up from the 2.6 percent growth the previous year."

Sigismondi attributes a good deal of that success to the rallying-to-gether response of the organization's personnel. "The pandemic environment brought people closer together at Dole. To me, it demonstrated the company's conviction to succeed. Our people in the factories worked remotely, packing and preparing labels in their houses. True to that, we are still experiencing great demand, especially for healthy, plant-based products."

Despite this all-for-one-and-one-for-all mentality, the physical and economic challenges presented by the pandemic were truly daunting. "As a leader, I could have never imagined a logistics environment that could eat up half my gross margin in sea freight costs alone," Sigismondi says. "It takes 30 percent more lead time to get a container loaded and delivered, and the cost is multiple times what it used to be. The rules have changed, as old contracts are not valid anymore. Planning accuracy goes for a toss, because it's a race for the most pragmatic way to land products on the shelf."

Regardless of their size, Sigismondi observes, companies have one cardinal duty: to manage demand and supply equations. "On the production side, we need to fulfill demand, and on the delivery side, we need to expand capacity. When an immense amount of working capital is locked up in inventories stuck on vessels or at port yards, it inevitably impacts your sales numbers due to [lack of] availability, and cramps you financially." On the other side of that coin, if, in their eagerness to improve customer service levels, companies end up holding more inventories than they could hope to sell, these excessive stockpiles will negatively impact cash flow — and, in a hot industrial real estate market, they could also significantly impact bottom lines due to rising storage costs.

The pandemic pointed to the need for supply chain leaders to maintain a balanced frame of mind that is uniquely tuned to solving problems. When Dole was faced with restrictions in industrial capacity, Sigismondi first looked at consolidation as a way to reduce the cost of capital post-pandemic, but soon realized that asset localization made more sense, as it pays to be close to the consumer.

"Being a distributed network is all about localization, which came at a higher cost in the early days," Sigismondi explains. "To secure financing is even more complicated if you're operating on a lower scale, like a local producer in the sub-region. But you significantly improve your responsiveness and product freshness. You're more localized and can build adaptive products to suit consumer needs. The spices and flavors coming from another country will not taste the same. It's about constantly striking the right balance."

That said, Sigismondi points out that "Localization could be more justified for some [companies] over others. For companies that bank heavily on intercontinental imports, localizing a part of their sourcing could build more resilience. On the other hand," he continues, "a company dealing in tropical fruit from the Caribbean cannot localize its sourcing from North America.

No matter a company's line of business, "You need to put all the key variables on your chart and think about balancing them all to create the best growth equation. It's not just about low cost — it's about achieving high growth that's also profitable. This means having the right product at the right time for consumers to pay a price that allows you to have the best gross margins. If that comes with a higher cost, so be it, because you deliver growth in volumes and gross margins."

BUILDING LASTING SUPPLY CHAINS WITH PURPOSE

"As a rule of thumb, I tell people that we need to do things in life that will get us out of bed every day," declares Sigismondi. "Is your purpose consistently compatible with what the company wants to achieve? And when you find that alignment and great chemistry, you're going to do your very best, and the results will soon follow."

Having transitioned across different roles over his career, Sigismondi believes that what makes leaders click is the clarity of purpose they bring to the table. "I started my career building airplanes, and today I'm selling bananas. You can make your job meaningful no matter what you do in life, how many people you lead, or which products you handle. It does not need to sound sexy to be meaningful and impactful for the world.

"As a person in the supply chain, you have an amazing advantage to go beyond your comfort zone, into areas like marketing and sales, and offer help, as you can learn more in areas that aren't your own."

To that point, Sigismondi firmly believes that to be a truly efficient leader who understands how the business operates at the leader-ship level, one must have a finance or supply chain background. "Only in these two roles are you entitled to work closely with every part of the business — be it in the innovation labs, on customer joint business plans, marketing a product with quality standards, or dealing with local regulations and taxes."

The head of the supply chain reserves the right to question different segments within the organization to support and drive the busi-ness. "The supply chain helps you observe the company closely and prepares you to manage it someday," says Sigismondi. "Being responsible for a business, I understand how important it is not just to be driven by the conventional carrot-and-stick leadership prin-ciples, but also to have meaningful conversations with the people running the day-to-day activities."

"Listening is the number one skill an outstanding C-suite professional must display with his board and executive teams. Only those who deeply listen can adapt and thrive in today's fast-changing world."

Given a supply chain leader's intrinsically strong connections to several stakeholders — both within and external to the company — it is critical that they ask relevant questions about how the business operates. "When you run a business yourself, you must learn how to ask the right question rather than only be concerned with having the right answer," Sigismondi says. In this regard, listening is the most essential and valuable skill that a leader can have, as it allows them to stay cognizant of different perspectives on and potential strategies for approaching a challenge.

"I start worrying when I see a key person in my team not asking questions, not taking notes, not looking at my eyes, or being distracted [by their own thoughts] while I talk," Sigismondi declares. "Listening is the number-one skill an outstanding C-suite professional must display with his board and executive teams. Only those who deeply listen can adapt and thrive in today's fast-changing world.

"Adaptability (AQ) comes way before IQ and EQ, in my view. And if you aren't convinced and still want to survive, read what Mr. Darwin said quite some years ago."

Scan the QR code below or visit www.sourcetosold.com to access exclusive bonus content you can use with your teams to further explore the concepts and insights covered in this book.

CHAPTER 24:

CLAUDIO STROBL

"Disruptive ideas are always coming your way — if you can't find them, it's because you're not challenging yourself enough."

Claudio Strobl is the senior vice president of operations at Kalmar, the largest business unit within Cargotec, a Helsinki-based firm that makes cargo and material-handling equipment for ships, ports, terminals and local distribution. Prior to joining Cargotec in 2019, he held a variety of senior positions in procurement, logistics, and supply chain as well as business area head at such global manufacturing companies as Volvo Construction Equipment (where he spent 25 years), Atlas Copco and Epiroc.

Despite Claudio's remarkable career in supply chain, he values sports and other facets in his life that are just as important to him as his career. "I love sports. I've played semi-professional soccer, higher-division badminton, I'm into running and road cycling, and just recently engaged in moderate-level track racing. But I also can hold my own with a guitar and cook you a great five-course dinner... maybe not at the same time though!" he laughs.

Strobl believes that, to a certain extent, the diversity of his interests may have helped him refine his leadership skills. "Leadership is about getting the best out of every person and of every team, sometimes in very challenging situations," he says. "That has helped me to stretch my boundaries and, more importantly, be positively inclined to do it, again and again. I believe that we grow as individuals, and, of course, as a team, when we push our boundaries and get out of our comfort zone. We need to. That's how kids learn. That's how we learn as adults. We just forgot how fun it was to learn something new."

"I believe great leaders must be positively charged and at all times ooze 'can do' and 'why not' attitude, inspiring teams to get the best out of each other and to really go for world-class," Strobl says. "Develop trust among the members of the team, encourage collaboration and empower everyone to believe that we really can be world-class, as there is no reason why not. It's an evolution — building a high-performing team doesn't just 'happen,' it's the execution of a well-structured plan. The team needs to desire and believe they can outperform and excel together."

Strobl singles out three key facets of leadership: sound listening skills, impeccable business acumen, and stellar people skills. "Leaders must be able to detect gaps in the business strategy, translate that into actionable items, and provide a clear business advantage to the organization," he says. "As far as supply chain goes, the ability to holistically assess the end-to-end supply chain and not just parts of it is key. This provides a window to opportunities for improving the entire supply or value chain, and avoid silo-thinking and sub-optimization throughout. That's really the name of the game, and a huge business opportunity."

AN OPEN APPROACH TO EXPLAINING THE SUPPLY-CHAIN BIG PICTURE

Strobl feels that supply chain leadership is obligated to help other parts of the organization understand the entire supply chain. "We live in a world with zillions of supply chains, and we interact with them every day. Everything we own and many services we enjoy are built around a form of supply chain. Competitive advantage in your supply chain could mean fulfilling your customer's order more efficiently than others in the market, which positively impacts the entire organization.

"I think we also haven't done a good job explaining our industry's complexity to anyone outside the supply chain. We haven't marketed ourselves well. Explaining complex supply chains to people without bringing them in is difficult, but still incredibly important."

"Transparency is the word — show everything, hide nothing."

For this reason, engagement with the company at large is crucial. "Be it sales, striking deals, or developing software applications, we can understand and solve complexities only if different segments within the company come together and actively participate in improvements," Strobl says. "The supply chain isn't an isolated field. It's a part of many services required to make a business function, and the more we open up to each other, the better we can run the business."

And this advice goes both ways: supply chains too need to be transparent in sharing data with other departments, which, Strobl argues, is often not the case. "Many functions, including supply chain, rarely share data, assuming people wouldn't understand. That's absolutely the wrong way to go about it, and only breeds distrust. Transparency is the word — show everything, hide nothing."

Strobl contends that supply chain practitioners have to take the role of enablers, bringing together suppliers, dealers, and customers. "We must take the liaising role and act as the glue that puts everyone in the business in context. For others to recognize our role, it starts with us and that we show the way by being totally open, transparent, and willing to collaborate at any time."

Staying true to his insistence on transparency and integration, Strobl will invite external partners, such as suppliers and dealers, to the company's S&OP meeting. "I fully believe that a game-changer in supply chain optimization is by bringing in all the major stakeholders in the process, and doing so as early as possible. That very much includes the external stakeholders like suppliers and dealers/customers. We are attempting to change our IBP (S&OP) process to 'CBP'— collaborative business planning, where external parties are also an integral part of the demand/supply balancing process.

"We start by inviting our key suppliers and explaining the context to them. We openly share our assembly build plans, and by doing so we gain the trust needed, leading suppliers to openly share their manufacturing plans and capacity/constraints in the same meeting. We can then optimize and build the business together, rather than individually, and overcome many bottlenecks and issues."

BUILDING A CULTURE OF COLLABORATION AND TEAM SPIRIT

"The primary thing I do is stay clear of micromanaging people," Strobl says. "Once we have agreed on the big goals, we need to allow them to think freely about how they want to tackle them. My contribution is to ensure that I free up the right resources and give people the time to involve themselves in solving such problems. I can't give people a monumental task on top of what they're already doing and force them to a great outcome. Instead, they need to be dedicated to the cause — which reflects our commitment and how serious we are about driving change toward the big goal.

"Of course, I do monitor progress, but more to ensure that I can support them properly — opening doors, removing obstacles, connecting them to best-practices benchmarks, and infusing [the] necessary skills to succeed. Once we agree on the target and timeframe, and the team feels empowered, I generally don't need to push them anymore. Without exception, people want to do a good job; so they deliver, and great things always come out of it."

DISRUPTIVE IDEAS ARE ALWAYS COMING YOUR WAY, BUT YOU NEED TO LISTEN TO FIND THEM

Strobl says that it is crucial to not always follow the fastest route to the desired result, if the goal is to adhere to sustainable outcomes. "I have a story to share from the early days of my career, when I went to work straight out of university. My manager had given me a small project to work on and report back with the findings. When I submitted the report, he looked right at me and asked me if this was the best I could do, without a single glance at the report. I replied in the affirmative, but he repeated [the question], and I started doubting myself.

"I took the report back and worked it over again, making it better and turning it in for the second time. The episode repeated again, and again. I spoke to my friends to get their view on the report in order to improve."

After four revisions, Strobl went back to his manager and stated that he had given his best, and there was nothing more he could do to improve the report. "The manager [opened] the report for the first time, and told me with a smile that things are hardly ever perfect when you do them for the first time, nor will they be in the second or third attempt — and certainly not if you only consult your own brain. You need to revisit your thoughts and conclusions by looking at things from many different perspectives. Other people can offer that opportunity — only then will the outcome be of the right quality and worthy of attaching your name to."

Strobl's manager proved his point, as this fourth report was miles better than the first one. "I think it's a powerful lesson," Strobl says. "Even today, I don't point out the obvious or potential wrongs [of a person's work] — instead, I merely challenge my teams by [asking] if they really have delivered their best work and stretched enough. Not surprisingly, they always come up with things that can be improved.

"Once you do this a few times, they come out of their comfort zone and go all out. And next time, they attack things differently. I think disruptive ideas are always coming your way — if you can't find them, it's because you are not challenging yourself enough."

It's for this reason that Strobl figures that supply chain leaders can make great CEOs. "When you're in the supply chain, you understand a large part of how the business and company practically work, and, ergo, also the obstacles you need to remove to achieve breakthrough. You master the problem-solving process needed to improve the overall business and the ultimate delivery experience for the customer.

"Supply chain leaders rising [through] the ranks to [become] CEOs will benefit the company, [as it] can blow past targets more efficiently with someone at the top who understands how things fit together in the end-to-end value chain, and how silo-thinking can be detrimental to any company. Good supply chain leaders know how to listen well and where to look for disruptive ideas that will change an industry."

STICKING TO BASICS WHEN HIRING PEOPLE AND MANAGING REDUNDANCIES

Another key area is, of course, to ensure the right team composition for your supply chain. "In general, I don't think leaders invest enough time and effort in this area — which is strange, as diversity has such a direct link to workplace satisfaction, and, of course, results," Strobl says.

Apart from the benefits to be accrued from having people of different ages, genders, and skill sets on your team, Strobl points out that another sector where you should seek out diversity is in the kinds of experiences your team members have had across the supply chain. Adding people with unique customer, dealer, or supplier experiences brings a competitive edge to your company, as too often the supply chain team lacks members that can provide authoritative input about the perspectives of these very important stakeholders.

While hiring is an integral part of being a supply chain leader, so is managing redundancies with worker numbers — a topic that is not spoken about as often as it should be. Strobl avers that some of the toughest moments in his career have been making decisions that led to the company parting ways with some of its people — not because of a given individual's performance or compliance issues, but because circumstances were such that the business took a wrong turn. "Giving people notice hurts me to the core," he says. "We as a company failed, and now these are the horrible consequences."

In a sunnier example of this worst-case scenario, Strobl relates an instance involving "a plant in a small city in Europe, with more than a hundred years of history and a sizable workforce in the community working in our plant — whole families were working there. When it was decided that we had to close the plant, I was part of the team ensuring the closure went smoothly, [which was] led by the plant manager and representatives of the municipality.

"We decided early on that we would not only let people go, but expand our mission to actively engage in getting everyone a new job, to the best of our ability. We spent time listening and talking to every employee, helping them write their resumes and upskill where needed. We went on to actively target and contact companies and suppliers we believed could be interested in establishing a presence in the existing facilities."

Right from day one, finding companies to fill up the facilities was never a problem. In the end, over fifty companies of various sizes were convinced to set up shop within the premises, and many of the employees who had been let go subsequently found new jobs there.

"Occasionally, I drive past the old factory area, and although it's twenty years since that happened, the place continues to be vibrant," Strobl says. "More companies have [a] presence there, and many of the existing ones have expanded. The town is much larger now. I feel proud that something good eventually came out of such a bad thing.

"I think it's important to realize that having a job is, in many aspects, a person's identity — [it's] their position or status in the community, and with [their] friends and family. As a leader, empathy and going the extra mile is crucial to create good outcomes for individuals and families involved with the company, and we owe it to our employees to put the effort in.

"Redundancies and letting people go was, to me, a hard experience. I don't want to put myself in that position if I can help it, ever again. Since then, I run a tight ship wherever I am, and I explain to my teams that this is the reason why I do it. I do my very best to be transparent at all times and ensure all levels in the company are aware of the company situation — for everyone to see and act upon. If there's a train coming, I want everyone in the company to see it in time and have the chance to change its course for the better. We all need to 'live the business' at all times — that has made a big difference on several occasions. Transparency is key in good times as well as in the bad times."

Scan the QR code below or visit www.sourcetosold.com to access exclusive bonus content you can use with your teams to further explore the concepts and insights covered in this book.

CHAPTER 25:

LYNN TORREL

"These two qualities are must-haves in any global leader: one, to ensure two-way communication; and two, to be clear about the strategies you're deploying and why you think they'll benefit the company in the long term."

Lynn Torrel is chief procurement and supply chain officer at global diversified manufacturer Flex, where she is responsible for direct and indirect materials, transportation and logistics, business operations, materials management and strategic supply chain management. Prior to joining Flex in 2019 she held several leadership roles at Avnet spanning global supply chain solutions, strategic accounts and semiconductor business development, among others.

When Lynn Torrel graduated with a bachelor's degree in communications and journalism, she had a career planned out that had little to do with supply chains. But when she ended up taking a job in distribution, she realized it was something she enjoyed working on. "The business side of things excited me," she says. "My aim in life has always been to develop myself and be on a path of continuous learning and growth. The supply chain gave me opportunities to do that and push myself to address industry challenges and develop successful strategies."

That said, her communications degree did come in handy, albeit much later in life as she climbed up the organizational ladder into supply chain leadership positions. "Having spent a lot of time in pan-European or global roles, I've understood communication is central to my job," Torrel says. For example, when she moved to Germany as manager of corporate account and logistics for EBV Elektronik, she realized she would have to drive business strategies and work with people for whom English was their second language. "You need to adapt your communication based on the people you work with. I consciously chose simpler words to get my point across, changing the way I spoke to ensure people from a non-English-speaking background understood what I was saying."

Torrel declares that what drives her in her job is plotting out growth strategies and scaling operations to global standards. "I approach my job by asking the right questions first. How can I bring value to this role? How do I evolve it? Finding answers to such questions eventually helped me create a positive influence on people reporting to me, and well beyond."

While at Avnet, she was asked to take the lead with a global customer based on her experience working in Europe. "Before I took the role, Avnet's growth was predominantly based on acquisitions, with all customer relationships being local," she explains. "With globalization occurring, numerous customers were requesting global support from Avnet. In developing our global strategies, I worked with my regional teams to see how we could adjust our approach to meet the requirements of the customer while driving increased revenue and improved processes for Avnet."

In Torrel's opinion, being nimble and malleable to change is what defines a good leader. "In 2015, at the height of the semiconductor revolution, my boss asked me to switch from managing our global customers and complex supply chain engagements to heading Avnet's global semiconductor supplier relationships. This was when the industry was consolidating, and much like our customers, our suppliers wanted to interface with Avnet globally. They wanted global contracts, terms and conditions, and were eager to set up global growth strategies."

Consequently, Torrel moved from managing a large team to being an individual contributor, and set about developing a model to support suppliers on a global basis. "I still look back on this experience as one of the most challenging roles I've ever taken, as it involved building a new framework for supplier management within a large global distributor. I took input from our regional leaders, openly asking them what they would focus on and how they would negotiate with the suppliers if they were in my shoes." Those discussions helped in the creation of a business model that enabled Avnet to meet the requirements of their supplier partners while also delivering increased market share, improved global processes, and upgraded growth strategies to the company.

This successful pattern would repeat itself as Torrel took on ever more roles. "Moving across different roles, I learned to develop different skill sets that allowed me to seek bigger challenges for our company and develop new, unique business models to address them. No matter what role I found myself in, be it managing a large team or working as an individual contributor, I made sure I led by influence instead of acting like a manager."

THE COMMUNICATION ASPECT OF SUPPLY CHAIN LEADERSHIP

Professional growth is a two-way street, Torrel asserts. "While I expect to have my team's support on meeting our metrics and implementing strategic initiatives, my team also wants to hear from me regarding the executive discussions I have on our performance and direction. I feel these two qualities are must-haves in any global leader: one, to ensure two-way communication; and two, to be clear about the strategies you're deploying and why you think they'll benefit the company in the long term. Clarifying this with the extended leadership team will help get them on board to work with you as new strategies are deployed."

Sustained communication was central to running supply chains during the height of the pandemic, when travel restrictions and local quarantines meant fewer face-to-face meetings. When the first wave of COVID-19 hit North America, Torrel had spent just about six months at Flex as its chief procurement and supply chain officer. While she had toured a few Flex facilities, met with the leadership teams, and conducted local town halls, that gradual integration process came to an abrupt halt as the sweeping, continent-wide restrictions took effect.

In response to these hobbling measures, "I made sure we continued to communicate within the organization as we made critical decisions, so I organized daily calls with my leadership team," Torrel recalls. "In addition, we had virtual town halls every quarter that connected my leadership team with the 10,000 people in procurement and supply chain at Flex. I sought ways to guarantee there was regular contact with the team to ensure operations ran seamlessly across our global supply chain during tough times.

"It was crucial to make certain everyone stayed updated on how we were performing, the critical challenges we were facing, and the strategies we were developing to manage the crisis. While travelling physically to meet our people in person was a great experience, remote connections gave me a medium to reach out to the larger audience effectively and quickly.

"We also changed the cadence of our quarterly newsletter on global procurement and supply chain to a weekly newsletter, as there was so much going on," Torrel continues. Two years after the onset of the pandemic, its impact persists — and so too do the weekly Flex newsletters. Torrel explains that such a well-thought-out combination of written and verbal communication guarantees the organization stays abreast of where it's heading and how it is making that happen.

Another part of the communication picture was the supportive message that Flex conveyed to its people during these fraught times. "When COVID was in its early stages and vaccines were yet to surface, I told my people that their families came first," Torrel says. "We acknowledged that we bear responsibility toward our loved ones, so I always encouraged them to take care of themselves and their family's mental and physical health. I pumped whatever energy I could through my words to help us manage through the crisis."

To that point, Torrel introduced a weekly happy hour initiative with her direct staff in March 2020 as a morale booster, which saw people meeting virtually every Monday. "We weren't allowed to bring up work topics, and this activity brought us closer in ways quarterly presentations and dinner get-togethers wouldn't," Torrel says. "We continued this ritual for quite a while, as it was a lighthearted, fun conversation all around. I received a unanimous agreement when I asked my staff if they wanted to continue the happy hours even after things got back to normal. So now we do it bi-weekly."

Another aspect of communication for supply chain professionals is how they get their point across to executives. Torrel stresses the need for brevity, as many executives do not come from a supply chain background and thus might find it hard to follow complicated logistics issues. "This is also true of other people you communicate with along the supply chain, such as suppliers and logistics providers," she adds. "You need to know how to be comprehensive enough without overwhelming people with unnecessary details. Concisely communicating the potential impact of a supply chain disruption and the actions being taken to mitigate that disruption is a required skill that is often overlooked, yet incredibly important for someone working in supply chain."

FORECASTING AND PREPARING FOR SUPPLY CHAIN DISRUPTION

"The supply chain is like a chessboard where you need to keep thinking of your next move while keeping real-time events in mind,"

Torrel contends. "It's never just about the immediate next step, but a complete outlook on the end-to-end supply chain. For instance, you may be able to secure the material, but there may be freight and logistics disruptions causing extended lead times. As a leader, you have to plan for and anticipate such situations, and react quickly to a disruption to adjust those plans to meet your requirements.

"The industry needs to focus on getting better at forecasting demand and dealing with disruptions. At Flex, we are continuously in discussions with our customers and suppliers about improving the ability to forecast supply and demand."

It is for this reason, Torrel argues, that supply chains are a long way from full automation. To accentuate the positive in what was a truly global crisis, the pandemic provided a lesson in how supply chains continue to be human-centered. The lockdown highlighted the importance of having a good rapport with your stakeholders in the value chain, as suppliers worked to support certain companies over others based on their relationships with the people within those organizations.

Another crucial benefit of keeping cognizant of external relations is that outward focus can give an organization early-warning data about potential trouble on the horizon, and allow it to respond in time. Torrel states that Flex uses every possible piece of information from every possible source — be it the media, government, customers, suppliers, or its own employees — to make sense of potential disruptions in its supply chain.

"I remember an incident where one of our people was driving to work, and he spotted a long queue to cross the border," Torrel recalls. "This was in Europe, and it instantly alarmed us, as we had our personal protective equipment (PPE) stored at a hub in Hungary, which would deliver to our European manufacturing locations, and we were moving this material in a just-in-time manner. With this observation [from the employee], we rushed to move all our PPE supplies out of the hub to the sites. Sure enough, the borders were shut a few days later." This is a cardinal example of supply chain professionals making an intelligent decision based on imperfect and anecdotal — but ultimately extremely valuable — data.

Torrel states that she is always focusing on finding the best possible way to manage Flex's broad supply base of over 16,000 suppliers. Pre-pandemic, just-in-time had been the guiding principle for many companies, with a focus on cost reductions and ensuring supplier programs worked seamlessly to create optimized procurement strategies. "The shift I see now is that pricing is no longer the central factor," contends Torrel. "Today, it's more about ensuring you have the required components to complete a build. Some of our customers are implementing resiliency strategies that involve designing in or approving alternate parts or holding buffer stock on critical components.

"There is a cost associated with [such measures], but while this does put pressure on an organization, companies need to look for strategies that will ensure an agile and resilient supply chain."

To that end, in 2015 Flex built a supply chain digitalization system that can provide real-time data visibility across its global supply chains. Dubbed the "Pulse Center," this homegrown system gathers information from all of Flex's systems worldwide and stores them in a central database. People needing to access information can swipe through various dashboards to look up the exact status of the delivery of a particular component.

"While we do have clear visibility into our first-tier and, to an extent, our second-tier suppliers, we need to do more to get visibility much further downstream," declares Torrel. "Mapping out and having full visibility across multiple tiers has always been a challenge. But we at Flex haven't stopped trying."

PLOTTING OUT A CAREER IN SUPPLY CHAIN MANAGEMENT

Improving as a supply chain leader requires obtaining a deeper understanding of how businesses and people interact. For Torrel, that learning came both on the job and through her studies for an MBA degree. "My MBA allowed me to put an academic context to my practical learnings, which helped differentiate me and round out my skill set and knowledge base," she says.

Equally critical is the need to stay constantly abreast of the happenings in the industry. Flex places an emphasis on internal training and equipping employees with development tools that help them stay at the cutting edge of supply chain innovation. Torrel makes a point of taking an interest in asking her people about their next career step, and encourages them to take responsibility for directing their careers.

"I discuss career aspirations with my employees, keeping in mind the strengths they can leverage going forward," she says. "I also talk to them about the areas I feel they need to work on, and suggest necessary tools or programs they can utilize to develop those required skills. These discussions are something every employee deserves from their manager. It also reflects the manager's eagerness to develop their teams."

Team development also involves charting out a succession plan. Torrel maintains that having a clear plan in place is key to effecting a seamless transition of power. "I've always emphasized the need for robust succession plans for my team and me. I like to have a successor identified and ready to step in. Otherwise, I cannot get promoted. Also, this allows the company to plan for and develop its future leaders."

Torrel is also an advocate for positive communication, citing it as a crucial quality in a leader. "I observe people's style of communication and their way of handling stress. Supply chains are a difficult place to work, and it can get quite stressful on the job. This makes it all the more important to communicate properly — whether good news or bad news — with customers, suppliers, and internal stakeholders. No matter the subject or the recipient, you need to be calm and transparent in your communications."

> "Whenever I'm presented with an opportunity, I question whether I can do this role successfully and approach it confidently. I go ahead only if I'm fully convinced that the answer to both of those questions is yes."

Correspondingly, Torrel disapproves of the use of aggressive communication as a show of strength, which some leaders believe can get them the results they're looking for. "That's not my style. I like to have a collaborative approach toward the people I'm dealing with."

That said, Torrel does advocate being bold and confident as a supply chain leader. "I've always been open to new opportunities, taking everything that comes to me as a learning experience. Whenever I'm presented with an opportunity, I question whether I can do this role successfully and approach it confidently. I go ahead only if I'm fully convinced that the answer to both of those questions is yes."

Being sensible about career moves is also crucial for people looking to rise up the ranks. Torrel spent 25 years at Avnet, and was president of a global business unit and managing their global supply chain at the time she made the jump to Flex. Although Avnet seemed like a dream job at that time, Torrel still made the transition as she saw more benefit in continuously learning and pushing her boundaries running procurement and supply chain operations for Flex.

"Moving to Flex from Avnet was a difficult decision. Like all other decisions in my career, I've never looked back on this one negatively. I don't have any regrets, and have increased my knowledge and skill set. I continue to look forward and try my best to bring value to my different roles, and this has served me well over the course of my career."

Scan the QR code below or visit www.sourcetosold.com to access exclusive bonus content you can use with your teams to further explore the concepts and insights covered in this book.

CHAPTER 26:

DONNA WARTON

"You can't lead others if you don't know yourself. You need to be self-aware of how you impact others, and stoke a desire to continue learning and grow to be the best version of yourself."

Donna Warton is the corporate vice president of Microsoft Windows + Devices supply chain and sustainability, managing the end-to-end supply chain for hardware, gaming and software including Surface, Surface Hub, HoloLens, Xbox, games and accessories. She also leads the sustainability efforts to reduce carbon and waste on products and the end-to-end supply chain. Prior to joining Microsoft, she served as VP of global operations at Dell and led the global supply chains for Mettler-Toledo International and Motorola's mobile device business.

Donna Warton has built herself a leadership portfolio that spans over three decades in the supply chain with stints at Microsoft, Dell, and Motorola. But she confesses that, to get to this level, she's had to sacrifice a lot of her weekends. "Most of my experiences have been leading transformations, which require executing the supply chain and at the same time transforming it," explains Warton, though she also notes that, earlier in her career, she scaled her work week down to four days and fewer hours so she could look after her two young daughters. Warton says that "Be there for the moments that matter to the ones you love" and "Make your job work with your life" are two principles she has adhered to throughout her career.

Asked to reflect on some signature moments from her supply chain experience, Warton recalls the launch of the RAZR cell phone during her time running the mobile devices supply chain at Motorola. "There were many obstacles to overcome to not just launch the phone, but also to scale it to a level unheard of before in the industry," she says. "The president of the mobile devices division [initially] set a target to sell one million phones a quarter, which then progressed to three million, six million, and then twenty million a quarter. It was my job to figure out how to deliver that volume.

"We soon realized that we wouldn't get anywhere by focusing on the twenty-million-a-quarter end goal, and figured we would have to break the target into smaller chunks to make it manageable. We did that, and within a year we were shipping ten million a month — and I specifically remember us shipping ten million units in one week, in December, 2006!"

Highlighting a different sort of supply chain challenge, Warton remembers that "when I took over the supply chain at Microsoft, the business grew, but we always had the wrong inventory. Sales and marketing were frustrated they couldn't get the products they wanted, and pushed to carry more inventory to solve the problem." But experience in operations led Warton to do the opposite: she implemented an inventory *reduction* target for her team, while simultaneously ensuring the supply chain could support business growth. Inventory reduction meant a laser focus on demand planning and supply response, pushing the team to whittle operating models down to the SKU level.

"While we didn't get it right every time, we built a predictable process that has helped grow the business significantly over the years," Warton says. "This is the ethos of the supply chain — it's a place where innovation meets execution. It's where demand and supply are rationalized. It's where big problems come to be solved."

THE BEHAVIORAL ATTRIBUTES THAT
DEFINE A SUPPLY CHAIN LEADER

"Everyone has moments in their life that shape them as a person and go on to define their set of values. These values become core to their way of leadership," states Warton. "Simply put, you can't lead others if you don't know yourself. You need to be self-aware of how you impact others, and stoke a desire to continue learning and grow to be the best version of yourself. My values have evolved over the years, and will likely continue to evolve."

One of the lessons Warton learned in her career is that it isn't enough to articulate what's possible or set a direction for your team — you have to follow through with your people to see if their perspectives, motivation, and ability align with the goal. "About a year into the digital transformation journey at Microsoft I saw that the team was frustrated with the tools and process changes, as they weren't making work easier," Warton says by way of example. "To many, using Excel was simpler. I chose to stop all work on the tool development, spoke to the team to reset our yearly goals, and refocused our efforts on a reduced scope.

"By meeting the team where they were, we proved the digital solution — albeit on a reduced scope — and scaled from there. In any transformation initiative, creating clarity to get from where you are to what success looks like and bringing others along is a powerful lesson in leadership."

Another leadership quality that Warton stresses is the ability to anticipate scenarios. "Anyone who is analytical and has an operational mindset has the potential to make it big in the supply chain. Analytical skills help you evaluate and understand trends vital to working in this industry. [For example], when I was at Motorola we lost about half a billion dollars a year, just in North America. Trends helped me anticipate early on that we needed to pivot our strategy, which eventually helped us stem the cash burn."

A key step in being able to anticipate market development is creating a performance and engagement plan. While no one knows how the future will actually play out, robust analysis of the situation will put data points into perspective and provide insights into what the future holds, allowing you to prepare the supply chain accordingly. "Learning from past experiences also helps craft better strategies for the future," adds Warton. "Analyzing what worked and what failed helps you create learnings that fuel better decision-making. As a supply chain leader, I spend a lot of time pondering ways to mitigate issues like material shortages and rate increases."

THE ESSENCE OF MAKING REAL, TANGIBLE CONNECTIONS

While Warton excelled as a supply chain leader during her stay at Motorola, she had not given much thought to expanding her network across the industry, save for connections within her organization. "It was only around the time I left Motorola that I realized this was something I had to work on," she says. "Being a woman also made it much harder for me to network in a male-dominated field. I had to leverage my work environment to reach out and build relationships. But I made the most of it. I talked to people about what my business was going through, shared what I was doing in my organization, and asked for advice unabashedly."

Warton explains that an essential part of networking is directly reaching out to people beyond your immediate network, as asking for advice and genuinely looking to make a connection with those outside your area of the business not only creates a good impression, but can help you to better realize your own goals. Warton recalls a time at Motorola when she was dealing with customers who were asking for volume discounts, but never truly followed through with their commitment to those order volumes even as they took advantage of the discounts. The supply chain team came up with an idea to stop asking for volume commitments from these customers and, instead, use the subsidized price slot as volume predictions, as this worked well to correlate to a retail price point.

"This meant that I had to convince the sales leaders to do a 180-degree shift on their negotiation strategy," Warton explains. After months of working on this idea and not getting traction, I realized the issue was not with our new strategy, but [with] my peers. They weren't listening to me because I hadn't built up any credibility with them. They viewed me as pushing an agenda, and they were the ones taking all the risk."

This led Warton to change her approach, as she began taking time to study and understand each account's sales process, challenges, and the issues customers face daily. "In three years, we went from losing $500 million a year to leading the market in profits. This reflects the need to be persistent and take feedback on what's working [in your approach] and what isn't. Most importantly, this underscores how changing your mindset from 'me' to 'we' can be miraculous in transforming a company's fortunes," she says.

"Networking is all about positioning yourself in the right way — asking for advice, getting educated, and requesting people to share their experiences. Most people are [willing] to help others if they see the right intentions."

BUILDING A TRULY DIVERSE ORGANIZATION

Warton considers herself lucky to be in the technology realm, where women are represented in higher numbers than in organizations entirely centered around supply chains. "The Microsoft devices supply chain has [a] nearly equal number of women as men, but in companies where you're the only woman in supply chain, it affects how you show up. The skewed ratio makes you self-conscious. On the flip side, having a diverse group of people around you expands your perspective. It gives you more confidence to speak up and engage." Warton contends that an ideal scenario would be for work teams to reflect the communities that their members live in, as an environment with diverse representation leads people to interact with each other as individuals.

Much of Warton's perspective on inclusivity goes back to the early days of her career, when she was frequently the only woman in meetings as well as the youngest person in the room. "I was in finance back then, and was the one who brought up difficult topics like slowing revenue growth, headcount reductions, and cost-cutting. I saw firsthand the impact on business results [from] leaders who welcomed and sought out diverse thoughts versus leaders who didn't. The cultural damage of having a fixed mindset ultimately impacts your bottom line, as you don't challenge assumptions. To echo Brené Brown, you care more about 'being right versus getting it right,' and worst of all, you miss out on the innovation and creativity from your employees to drive business success."

Warton argues that attracting more women and minorities to your workforce should not simply be about hitting equality benchmarks — companies need to ensure that these valuable human resources also feel included and heard. "It hasn't always been this way, and it's time to change that. We must also take conscious steps to recruit and retain a diverse workforce at every level," she says.

"Today, we see a good number of women early on in their careers, but not so many advancing to the middle and higher levels. Hiring a diverse workforce that stays requires hard work and meticulous planning that you must be willing to put in as a leader. You have to create the right roles to give them space to learn and grow, and provide [them with a] purpose to stay in the company."

Implementing change in the organization can start with policies, which can be scaled up to include everyone due to its positive impact. For instance, expanding the gender requirements on mater-nity leave to include paternity leave as well has greatly improved work-life balance for young families. Many companies have also now introduced family leave allotments to support employees who have to take care of a loved one.

"While giving people options is the first step, leaders [also] need to show support for these policies to make them work for [both] the individual and the organization," Warton argues. "[For example], I had a boss that promoted me after I came back from maternity leave. That was a risky move for him, but he showed the team that taking the time for a life event doesn't mean it has to slow your career trajectory.

"These things look easy on paper, but it will take action from leaders to make them culturally acceptable."

UNLOCKING THE FUTURE OF SUPPLY CHAIN THROUGH MULTI-TIER VISIBILITY

As supply chains grow to prioritize visibility as a vital metric in an environment of continuous disruption, organizations are turning to data-based insights for support — a trend that Microsoft, as a frontrunner in the tech field, naturally falls into. "Five years ago, we began a journey to maximize visibility across the end-to-end supply chain, and we've achieved 90 percent visibility with a 99.5 percent data accuracy," Warton says. "We've attained comprehensive visibility into our Tier 1 suppliers, progressing to our Tier 2 and Tier 3 suppliers — all the way to the customer shelf.

"Treating data like an asset, such as inventory, is critical. At Microsoft, we take great pains to ensure data is complete, correct, and available on time."

Warton presides over a team that continuously updates its data management techniques and systems, with metrics evolving to incorporate new capabilities mushrooming in the space. "I place importance on the capability and the skill-set piece of the puzzle," she states. "We're investing in people that come with data science skills. Of course, we don't need everyone to have a master's in data science, but our people need to understand data architecture and ways to access and process data. I believe that every job description in the supply chain needs to include data analytics. Everyone, from the factory workers to the top managers, needs upskilling to match today's degree of digitalization."

While these changes at Microsoft were imminent, the timeline for implementation was considerably shortened due to the chipset supply issues brought about by the pandemic. Warton contends that the crisis made companies realize the need to change their procurement processes and put greater significance on inter-tier visibility.

"People were forced to think and plan months ahead. We had to look at the substrate stats to determine if we would get the part we needed on the product at the right time. Many decisions needed to be made in advance — be it more sources for particular parts, increasing purchase order volumes, or locking in agreements to ensure guaranteed capacity. This involved coordination across the enterprise, partnering with customers on their needs and [with] suppliers to ensure they understood what we needed and when.

"Supply chain professionals are the orchestrators to optimize execution, especially when dealing with disruptions."

SEEING THE BIG PICTURE AMID SUPPLY CHAIN CHAOS

For Warton, the mark of a good leader is to be unfazed by big problems. "Don't shy away from challenging roles," she advises. "In every role you take up, think about what you want to learn and how you can make that role better. I always thought of ways to leave my mark — I didn't do this to prove something, but as a way to satisfy expectations I set for myself."

While opportunities may be hard to come by, grabbing them when they appear gets your foot in the door. Warton says that her first consideration in those times when she was looking for a new role would be to see the impact she could have on the business. As she went up the ladder her challenges got bigger, and so did the stakes — but even early in her career, she was able to locate those inflection points where she could make a difference.

"When I was in finance, the in-transit inventory across many factories I supported were not reconcilable," she recalls. "I brought people together across functions, and after a two-day session we realized where the issues were. It ended up being a write-off, but it [wasn't] in vain — we improved the processes to avoid future write-offs and enabled people to be part of the transformation, to learn, and have a sense of accomplishment."

> "In every role you take up, think about what you want to learn and how you can make that role better.... Focus on the impact, and don't let a title or the size of your team discourage you from taking a role."

A career in supply chain can see many curve balls thrown at you, and Warton believes that a potential leader must be happy to engage with that host of troubles as they arise. "People think about their career journey in linear terms, with annual promotions, a bigger title, and progression in the size of the team they manage. This is a mistake. Focus on the impact, and don't let a title or the size of your team discourage you from taking a role.

"When I entered the tech world 25 years ago, it was at its nascent stages, and I was solving problems never touched before. While people from the US worked domestically, I chose to go global. Do not limit your career — try moving away from the status quo. Ultimately, when you look back after a long, fulfilling career, you'll find yourself having pushed boundaries that many thought were impossible."

Scan the QR code below or visit www.sourcetosold.com to access exclusive bonus content you can use with your teams to further explore the concepts and insights covered in this book.

THE CHAIN MODEL: LAYING THE FOUNDATION FOR FUTURE SUPPLY CHAIN LEADERS

If you've learned just one lesson from the conversations in this book, it's hopefully that there's no *one* path to success in supply chain. Our contributors come from varying personal and professional backgrounds, came into supply chain through a wide range of routes, and have had different kinds of experiences in very different cultural and geographical contexts.

But as both we and, hopefully, you noticed when reading these conversations, there are some very pronounced echoes and shared convictions running through each one. So as we conclude this book, we'd like to offer you a (very) condensed "formula" for what it takes to be a successful supply chain leader.

We call this the CHAIN model, which stands for:

Collaborative. A supply chain leader needs to build relationships, not simply manage transactions. You need to view everyone at every stage of that chain as your colleagues in a common cause.

Within your own team, foster a culture of questioning that allows your reports to bring their own opinions, observations and expertise to the fore. Be confident in your own ideas, but flexible enough to incorporate insights and input from your team.

Outside your team, bring other departments and external partners into your planning process. Be open and transparent with these partners about what you are trying to accomplish and how you are going about it, and invite them to do the same. Aligning across the chain by way of collaboration will not only optimize processes, but also build an invaluable base of trust.

Holistic. Don't fall victim to silo-thinking. Understand that supply chain is the link between a network of services, functions and interests, and assess and appreciate what is required at each stage of that journey. When you develop a true end-to-end comprehension of how supply chain gets a product from source to sold, you have a panoramic picture of your business as a whole.

A supply chain leader needs to be multi-dimensional — you need to have operational, data, analytical, technological, and above all people skills. BUT remember that you're not going to acquire all these at once. You need to continually expose yourself to other areas, disciplines, skills, ideas, and *people* by networking with peers, reading books and articles, and seeking insights from other fields that have value for your own. Commit yourself to lifelong learning.

And as part of that learning, work to foster *diversity* across your team — not only of ethnicity and gender, but also of age and experience. The wider and deeper the pool, the more you will have to draw from.

Adaptable. By which we could also say *actionable*. A supply chain leader needs to be both efficiently reactive in a crisis, and proactive in perceiving the possibility of future crises and preparing mitigation strategies.

Work towards a system that is resilient and agile enough to not only cope with crises, but convert them into opportunities. Don't be lulled by the calm and evenness of the day-to-day: be constantly on the alert for gaps, flaws, failings and loose connections, and devise ways to minimize or eliminate them before they can wreak their damage.

Influential. This needs to go both up and down the ladder. For your team, you first need to establish a connection. Sharing personal stories that will *resonate with the character of your team and the nature of the work environment* is a great way to start breaking down barriers and build a common purpose.

You need to communicate supply chain's mission clearly and powerfully to your team so that they understand not just the mission, but their own roles within it. *Don't micromanage* — empower your team members to take the initiative within the framework you've set out, and encourage them to work with their peers to find the best solutions. Through your own attitude, show them that there's no reason that the team *shouldn't* accomplish its goals and targets with the talent and knowledge it contains.

For leadership, you need to *tell the supply chain story in language they can understand*. For this audience, go for the broad strokes rather than fine details — use analogies, stories, visuals rather than numbers and dates to show them just how vital supply chain is to fulfilling the promise on which the business is built (without slighting any of the other critical sectors, of course!).

No matter what the audience, always *communicate, communicate, communicate*. And what you are communicating is…

Narrative. Or "vision," or whichever term you prefer. No one is inspired by *functions* — what inspire us are *stories*, and storytelling is perhaps the most important skill you need to master as a leader. When your team members, partners and collaborators can see themselves as *characters* within a story that is bigger than themselves, they not only buy into that narrative but can also be motivated to go beyond what they thought were their limits. And when leadership understands that supply chain is not simply numbers on a spreadsheet but a *living story* that is the lifeblood of their business, they can see that it has much to tell them about both where that business is and where it's going.

It's important to remember that the model above is *not* some step-by-step guide to success — it's a roster of *principles*, or *values*, or *qualities* that we've seen in so many of the top-flight leaders interviewed for this book. One of the joys of supply chain is that nearly every business' version of it is going to have a different shape, different components, different processes and different challenges, which means that, as a leader, you can customize it to your unique demands. But we believe that the sketch we've offered above encompasses much of what has allowed the greatest leaders in the field to reach the heights they have — and they can do the same for you.

Wherever your supply chain journey takes you, we hope that the stories in this book can serve as both an inspiration and a guide. And we would love to further accompany and aid you on that journey through the Alcott Global Academy, where we translate the wealth of knowledge and experience that the book's contributors generously provided into a practical program of instruction, enrichment and career counseling.

Thank you for reading *From Source to Sold*. We hope that you found the stories of these exceptional leaders as fascinating and inspiring as we did.

Be sure to scan the QR code below or visit www.sourcetosold.com to access exclusive bonus content you can use with your teams to further explore the concepts and insights covered in this book.

ABOUT THE AUTHORS

RADU PALAMARIU

Radu Palamariu is the managing director of Alcott Global, the leading global executive search firm focused on operations and supply chain. He works on global C-level assignments with Fortune 500 companies and local conglomerates, particularly in the areas of manufacturing, logistics, transportation, supply chain management and e-commerce.

A frequent speaker at industry conferences across the world, Radu is a contributor to the latest technologies shaping supply chains, as well as human resources trends and developments. He is also the host of the *Leaders in Supply Chain* podcast, which is consistently ranked among the top five industry podcasts globally.

Radu has been featured in the World Economic Forum, *Bloomberg*, *Forbes* and the *MIT Supply Chain Talent Magazine*, and is ranked as one of the top three global supply chain influencers on LinkedIn.

KNUT ALICKE

Knut Alicke is a partner and head of supply chain for Europe at McKinsey & Company, where he advises clients on a variety of topics, including supply chain management, digital supply chains, advanced analytics, and supply chain transformations. He is also a visiting professor of supply chain at the University of Cologne, a global expert on the topics of operations, supply chain, and risk, and was ranked as one of the top three supply chain influencers by a supply chain magazine.

Knut has written several articles on subjects related to supply chain, and is the author of a highly regarded book on supply chain management, *Planning and Operation of Logistics Networks: Cross-Company Supply Chain Management* (published in German).

ABOUT THE EDITOR

VISHNU RAJAMANICKAM

Vishnu Rajamanickam is a transport and logistics journalist specializing in the North American maritime and trucking segment. He is a contributing journalist to *Business Insider*, and an editor of supply chain for Reuters Events. Previously, he worked at the supply chain media company FreightWaves, where he became the outlet's first freight tech reporter.

Vishnu primarily writes commentaries on supply chain trends, works on market data reports, profiles start-ups, and brings in perspectives from thought leaders in the space. He also runs a content consulting business in the supply chain niche, where he works with companies ranging from scale-ups to publicly traded incumbents.

ACKNOWLEDGMENTS

This book is the result of a concerted effort of a number of people, who either directly or indirectly helped make this book possible.

Interviews with numerous friends and business partners encouraged the idea of this project coming to life, therefore we would like to mention many of those who believed in this initiative and supported us through the aforementioned journey, in no particular order: Dan Swan, Axel Karlson, Sanne Manders, Inna Kuznetsova, Saskia Groenin't-woud, Thomas Knudsen, Andreu Marco, Hannah Kain, Jaya Mittal, Norman Mummery, Dimitri Tsamados, Sabine Mueller, Fabrice Thomas, Christian Bonnet, Farzana Shubarna, Charles Brewer, Daniel Stanton, Beth Morgan, Wei Chuen Chua, Ghim Siew Ho, Paul Good, Anders Nordahl, Manuel Purwin, Tia Mohan, Ruben Huber, Andrew Bryant, Andreas Radke, Yasmine Khater, Alberto Hausmann, Bruno Sidler, Francisco Betti, Sheri Hinish, Stephan de Barse, Jerome Remeur, Samuel Tamagnaud, Angelo Cenon Valdez, and Charles Henri Dumon.

We would also like to thank the entire business development team at Alcott Global: Andrei Palamariu, Fei Yu, Rushit Shah, Crystal Poh, Rosalie Nunsol and Gina Paragas for their commitment to discovering the right talents among the supply chain industry for our clients as well as identifying their needs and coming up with the idea of this project, after so many inspirational discussions.

Naturally, we feel like all book contributors should once again be mentioned, as their stories are destined to inspire future generations of Supply Chain leaders. Thank you for being so supportive throughout this journey: Vikram Agarwal, Essa Al-Saleh, Ken Allen, Michael Corbo, Achim Dünnwald, Bonnie Fetch, Deepak Garg, Dirk Holbach, Ivanka Janssen, Andreas Krinninger, Jay Lee, Sandra Mac-Quillan, Tan Chong Meng, Sascha Menges, Sami Naffakh, Thomas Netzer, Ernest Nicolas, Tommy Nielson, Beatrix Praeceptor, Chouaib Rokbi, Jim Rowan, Yossi Sheffi, Pier Luigi Sigismondi, Claudio Strobl, Lynn Torrel, and Donna Warton.

Furthermore, we'd like to give a huge thank you to the marketing teams at Dole, Rivigo, PSA, MIT, Mondelez, Rockwell Automation, Colgate Palmolive, Foxconn, Cummins, Microsoft, Flextronics, Philips, Husqvarna, Vestas, Reckitt, KION, Wayfair, Royal Mail, Volvo, DHL, Mondi, Volta, Henkel, Danone, ST Microelectronics and Cargotec, for helping us share the news about this great project on their various social media platforms.

We would like to thank Ruchi Das, for her dedication in editing the interview transcripts on a tight schedule, Vishnu Rajamanickam for finding and refining the right tone of voice for the entire manuscript, and to Andrew Tracy for adding the final touches to it. Thank you to Grammar Factory Publishing, especially to Scott MacMillan for coming up with strategic input regarding the book launch strategy and to Christian Johnson for aligning everyone involved in this project.

Thank you to Cristina Tetcu for her tireless efforts building a great team and to the marketing team – Bryan Sombilon, Charlene Campos, Gretiel Sotelo, Jean Pagalan, Rheven Domo Virtudazo, and to Claudia Marta for her marketing, public relations and events skills – their contribution was essential to making this project a reality and getting the worldwide exposure it deserves.

Thank you to Shub Faujdar and Fei Wu for co-ordinating the development of exclusive content for the book's readers, which offers tools for leaders to upskill their teams and ignite meaningful conversations within their teams using this great compendium of stories as a springboard. This offers a great way for the book to stay relevant for years to come and provide inspiration to the great supply chain community and beyond.

We invite all you to visit our Alcott Global Academy web page at www.alcottglobal.com/alcott-global-supply-chain-academy/ to discover more content that would help you grow in your career or your business.

Lastly, we would like to give a huge thank you to all our readers. Thank you for reading this book, thank you for sharing and recommending this book, and thank you for bringing this book to life by sharing it within your teams and sparking debate about our CHAIN model for supply chain leadership.

We trust that this book will help you both now and in your future endeavors.

Get out there and make a dent in the world!

Radu and Knut

P.S. As we think of ourselves as connectors of the supply chain community, we would love to hear from you about how this book helped and what you enjoyed most about it. We'd love to receive photos with you and your teams talking about the stories we've shared here and how they inspired you. And we'd also love to learn about all the stories *you* create as you put the lessons from this book into practice. We're here to listen and grow this community together.

For enquiries, e-mail us at radu@sourcetosold.com and knut@sourcetosold.com.

ABOUT ALCOTT GLOBAL

Alcott Global is the leading end-to-end supply chain executive search, training and development solution provider for the world's top companies in manufacturing, e-commerce, logistics, and technology in supply chain. Our global projects span North America, Latin America, the Middle East, Europe and Asia – all of which have unique regional challenges that must be addressed. Alcott Global is a long-term partner for its clients in attracting, retaining, and developing supply chain talent. Recent projects include the launch of the Alcott Global Supply Chain Academy (www.alcottglobal.com/alcott-global-supply-chain-academy) and the Supplify platform (www.getsupplify.com), which are examples of initiatives that enable us to be true to our vision of connecting and upgrading the supply chain ecosystem.

Alcott Global PR Contacts

Claudia Marta, Senior Marketing, PR & Events Director
claudia@alcottglobal.co

Cristina Tetcu, Head of Global Partnerships & Marketing
cristina@alcottglobal.co

ABOUT MCKINSEY & COMPANY

McKinsey & Company is a global management consulting firm committed to helping organizations accelerate sustainable and inclusive growth. We work with clients across the private, public, and social sectors to solve complex problems and create positive change for all their stakeholders. We combine bold strategies and transformative technologies to help organizations innovate more sustainably, achieve lasting gains in performance, and build work-forces that will thrive for this generation and the next.